The five chapters that make up this short book examine the love elegies of the Roman poets Tibullus, Propertius and Ovid from the point of view of the way the meanings attributed to the poems arise out of the interests and preoccupations of the cultural situation in which they are read. Each study is centered around a reading of a poem or poems together with a discussion of a variety of sophisticated theoretical approaches drawn from modern scholars and theorists such as Paul Veyne, Roland Barthes and Michel Foucault. In each case, the modes of analysis involved are pressed hard to see where they may lead, and, equally, where they may show signs of strain. All Latin texts and terms are translated or closely paraphrased.

Although the book concentrates on the work of the Roman elegists, the challenging insights it offers into the processes involved in the reading and appropriation of the texts of the past are relevant to scholars and students of classical literature in general, and its discussion of such key issues as history, textuality, representation, discourse, gender, ideology and metaphor will be of concern to those interested in literary theory and cultural studies.

ROMAN LITERATURE
AND ITS CONTEXTS

The arts of love

ROMAN LITERATURE
AND ITS CONTEXTS

Series editors:
Denis Feeney and Stephen Hinds

The editors of this series share the growing belief that the dominant modes of study of Roman literature are insufficiently in touch with current research in other areas of the classics, and in the humanities at large. Students of Greek literature, in the best traditions of classical scholarship, have been strengthening their contacts with cognate fields such as social history, anthropology, history of thought, linguistics and literary theory; the study of Roman literature has just as much to gain from engaging with these other contexts and intellectual traditions. The series is designed to encourage readers of Latin texts to sharpen their readings by placing them in broader and better-defined contexts, and to encourage other classicists to explore the general or particular implications of their work for readers of Latin texts. The books all constitute original and innovative research and are envisaged as suggestive essays whose aim is to stimulate debate.

Other books in the series

Philip Hardie, *The epic successors of Virgil: a study in the dynamics of a tradition*

Charles Martindale, *Redeeming the text: Latin poetry and the hermeneutics of reception*

The arts of love

Five studies in the discourse of Roman love elegy

Duncan F. Kennedy

*Lecturer in Classics,
University of Bristol*

CAMBRIDGE
UNIVERSITY PRESS

Published by the Press Syndicate of the University of Cambridge
The Pitt Building, Trumpington Street, Cambridge CB2 1RP
40 West 20th Street, New York NY 10011-4211, USA
10 Stamford Road, Oakleigh, Victoria 3166, Australia

First published 1993

Printed in Great Britain at the University Press, Cambridge

A catalogue record for this book is available from the British Library

Library of Congress cataloguing in publication data

Kennedy, Duncan F.
The arts of love: five studies in the discourse of Roman love
elegy / Duncan F. Kennedy.
p.   cm. – (Roman literature and its contexts)
Includes bibliographical references and index.
ISBN 0 521 40422 3 (hardback). – ISBN 0 521 40767 2 (paperback)
1. Elegiac poetry, Latin – History and criticism.   2. Love poetry.
Latin – History and criticism.   I. Title.   II. Series.
PA6059.E6K46   1993
871'.0109354 – dc20   91–46973   CIP

ISBN 0 521 40422 3 hardback
ISBN 0 521 40767 2 paperback

et multi, quae sit nostra Corinna, rogant
Ovid, *Ars amatoria* 3.538

Contents

Preface

The five studies which make up this book are each built around a theme (representation, essentialism, metaphor, discourse and identification) which I have found useful in organizing my response to the texts of elegy and the types of reading they have recently evoked. Though the studies are nominally separate, key issues will be found to recur again and again. In particular, in a book written for a series entitled 'Roman Literature and its Contexts', I have tried to keep in mind the continuing need to examine the question of the historical sitedness of both the texts of elegy and the readings in which their meaning is realized here and now. Each chapter is centred around a reading of a poem or poems together with a discussion of those modern critics who in one way or another have something interesting to say which bears on the ways elegy is currently read. In each case I have tried to press their modes of analysis to see where they may lead, and, equally, where they may show signs of strain.

Acknowledgements

Love's atopia, the characteristic which causes it to escape all dissertations, would be that *ultimately* it is possible to talk about love only *according to a strict allocutive determination*; whether philosophical, gnomic, lyric, or novelistic, there is always, in the discourse upon love, a person whom one addresses, though this person may have shifted to the condition of a phantom or a creature still to come. No one wants to speak of love unless it is *for* someone.   (Barthes 1979, 74)

These observations from Roland Barthes' *A Lover's Discourse* come fittingly just before his discussion of 'The Dedication', and they are appropriate also to the dedication I have made. There are many people without whom I would never have been brought to ponder the issues in the way that I have in this book, and not all of them can be named in this acknowledgement. I owe much to my students, especially Damaris Barber, Deirdre Healy, Alex Langdon and Terry McKiernan, for always keeping me thinking, and to John Henderson, for never, over many years, allowing me to stop, and for showing me an unpublished piece on Ovid, *Amores* 2.7 (to appear in *Materiali e discussioni*). In helping me to turn my thoughts into a book, Denis Feeney, Stephen Hinds and Pauline Hire have played their various editorial roles to real perfection. A number of people were kind enough to read my drafts, and their reactions have helped to shape the final version. I am grateful to Alison R. Sharrock for her help at the initial stage and beyond, and to Catharine Edwards for her penetrating insights; Maria Wyke's presence informs this work more than the bare references to her writings might imply. My greatest debt is to the support I have derived from the constant criticism of Charles Martindale, that most determined of enablers, without whom the idea for this book would not have arisen, let alone come to a conclusion. Their generous and good-humoured forbearance has turned this *Tractatus Erotico-Philologicus* into a labour of love.

Representation and the rhetoric of reality

The notion of representation plays a prominent role in aesthetic criticism. The relational sense of the term, that of 'representing', 'standing for', opens up a characteristic disjunction, expressed as between 'art' and 'the world', or 'literature' and 'life'. Another character-istic distinction generated by the term is that between the 'means' and the 'object' of representation. The capacity of representational art to elide these disjunctions, indeed the projection of this on occasions as an ideal of such art, is remarked upon in the story of Pygmalion in Ovid's *Metamorphoses*: Pygmalion creates an ivory statue with such skill that he comes to think of it as a flesh-and-blood woman, 'to such an extent does artistry lie hidden by means of its own artistry' (*ars adeo latet arte sua*, 10.252). From the perspective of semiotics (the discourse of the sign, which also invokes representation as a foundational concept in its assertion that a sign 'stands for' something else), Roland Barthes has treated in detail of the means by which a text can draw attention away from itself as text so as to create the 'reality effect', the sense of direct contact with the real.[1] Contrariwise, the distinction between means and object can lead to emphasis on the former (formalism), as the represented object recedes whilst the medium turns itself back on its own codes and conventions and engages in self-reflexive play. As is the case with all terms projected as autonomous opposites, these distinctions are open to deconstruction, but generate meaning to the extent to which, in what ways, and to what ends, they are kept distinct. Texts work within such distinctions, even when they endeavour to collapse them. Criticism and its object, often projected as separate, can also be seen as operating

[1] Barthes (1974).

within similar assumptions and implicated in the same discursive strategies, by viewing them as two examples of 'the same thing', as, say, 'kinds of writing'; their very projection as separate instances of discrete phenomena can be one of the means whereby this complicity is disguised.

The terms of this discourse of representation are much in evidence in current discussion of Roman love elegy. In the Introduction to his *Latin Poets and Roman Life*, Jasper Griffin locates himself within this discourse and adopts a particular perspective:

> This book aims to illustrate and clarify the relationship between Augustan poetry and the world in which it was produced and enjoyed. Many readers of Augustan poetry have difficulty with an obvious and central feature: the highly polished verbal style and the brilliant metrical expertise are accompanied by highly stylised conventions of situation and attitude. Yet behind the conventional devices – the pastoral scenes, the songs sung outside closed doors, the Greek myths – the reader feels the presence of emotional truth. How is this effect produced, and what is the relation of the finished poem to the raw stuff of life?[2]

The particularly sharp distinction drawn here between 'poetry' and 'the world' generates its own problematic, the 'relationship' between the 'means' (the highly polished verbal style, the highly stylized conventions of situation and attitude, the conventional devices, the finished poem) and the 'object', which is also the ostensible *object*, the end, of the enquiry, the raw stuff of life, the achievement of which is signalled by the term 'presence'. The verbal texture of the poetry is thus presented as a barrier; Griffin's text holds out the hope of passing through that barrier to achieve a direct experience of reality. Drawing attention to the problems posed by the formal texture of Augustan poetry serves to suppress the involvement of Griffin's own text in the rhetorical strategies of representation he seeks to describe: under what circumstances will we be deemed to be in the 'presence' of 'reality'? At what point will the verbal texture of Griffin's own text claim to have elided itself?

In the course of discussing 'Augustan poetry and the life of luxury', Griffin asks of Horace, *Odes* 1.17: 'Is this musical *fête champêtre* a transparent fiction?'[3] He thinks it is not, and that 'we can trace it through a less exalted stylisation to reality'. Adducing *Odes* 2.11.13ff., he

---

[2] Griffin (1985), ix.　　[3] Griffin (1985), 20.

remarks: 'Here we are less grand: here alone in the *Odes* the low word *scortum* appears . . . Yet the ingredients are all the same: a girl, music, drink, in the country.' As further evidence, it is stated that:

> we come down to realism in Ovid's account of the holiday in honour of Anna Perenna, *Fasti* 3.523 ff.: on the banks of the Tiber,
>
>> plebs venit ac virides passim disiecta per herbas
>>   potat, et accumbit cum pare quisque sua
>
> 'The common people come and lie about on the grass and drink, each man stretched out with his girl' . . . This unromantic and plebeian scene is, presumably, 'realistic' enough, and shows that one could have a picnic in Augustan Italy without becoming a poetical fiction.

The progressive condescension ('Here we are less grand'; 'the low word *scortum*'; 'we come down to realism'; 'this unromantic and plebeian scene is presumably "realistic" enough') tends to associate reality with, and seeks to find it in, the *plebs*, the common people. But Griffin resists using the word 'reality' here, preferring for the moment 'realism' and 'realistic', the latter betraying some anxiety by its enclosure within inverted commas. When the 'reality effect' is working, the text seems to be elided and the reader seems to belong to the world depicted; conversely, the invocation of the term 'realism' indicates, albeit expressed as a residual awareness of the act of representation, both a sense of fascination for what is depicted and of being an observer rather than a participant, of 'seeing', perhaps, rather than 'being present'. The works of Petronius and Juvenal, which are often held to depict a world peopled by lower social groups and viewed from their perspective, are constantly praised for their 'realism'. Critics who use the term project themselves as interlopers, however much they enjoy the temporary frisson of seeing how the other half lives from the safe confines, and through the window, of a racy textual vehicle. The milieu of Augustan poetry is, by contrast, characterized as predominantly aristocratic, and the world it depicts as viewed from that perspective. 'The poem then', Griffin concludes as he safely returns to *Odes* 1.17, 'is not a fantasy in no relation to life, a "dream", but a stylised and refined version of reality.' In the word 'refined', which seamlessly combines the discourses of artistic and social differentiation, Griffin finds the reassuring sense of 'presence' which licenses the use of the master term 'reality'. And curiously, those very conventional devices which were projected as a barrier to reality are now coming to take on the role of reality, a critical position Griffin is elsewhere very keen to distance himself from when he discusses 'Genre and real life in Latin poetry'.[4] Curiously too, the act of emphasizing the fundamental difference between the musical *fête champêtre* and the plebeian picnic, the difference which is held to constitute reality, has involved the projection of the two as instances of the same thing . . .

The strategy of grounding 'reality' in a discourse of social and aesthetic differentiation whilst the author coalesces with a point of view emerges again when Griffin turns to contemplate the pleasures of nakedness. Discussing devices to justify the representation of naked women (the bath and the presence of molesting satyrs are the examples adduced),[5] Griffin observes that 'the application to the nude of some trappings of mythology could make a great difference to its respectability', and points to Alma Tadema's Roman ladies in the bath and Lord Leighton's Greek nudes to suggest the similarity of Victorian practice.[6] He suggests a similar dignifying function for Propertius' use of the Judgement of Paris to suggest the beauty of Cynthia in 2.2.13–14:

> cedite iam, divae, quas pastor viderat olim
> Idaeis tunicas ponere verticibus

> Yield now, you goddesses, whom once the shepherd saw undress on Mount Ida

He adduces the parallel of *Ars* 1.247–8[7] as Ovid drawing 'the frank moral from the story that, as Paris looked the goddesses over thoroughly before making his choice, so his male readers, too, should look carefully before choosing a girl', which leads immediately to the following reverie: 'the picture of a Roman man about town, running an eye over the girls on offer in some louche establishment, is almost tangibly present'.[8] The rhetorical strategy underpinning the discourse of 'reality', culminating in the phrase 'almost tangibly present', is by now familiar. The perspective adopted (explicitly figured in terms of 'running an eye over') is that of a 'man about town' visiting 'some louche establishment' – overtly male,

[4] Griffin (1985), 49.   [5] Griffin (1985), 103.   [6] Griffin (1985), 104.
[7] *luce deas caeloque Paris spectavit aperto,|cum dixit Veneri 'vincis utramque, Venus'.* ('Paris viewed the goddesses in broad daylight when he said to Venus "You beat them both, Venus".')   [8] Griffin (1985), 105.

overtly privileged. But what Griffin holds out to us here is not reality but, explicitly, a *picture*, another representation, just as, in retrospect, the musical *fête champêtre* of Horace, *Odes* 1.17 was a stylized and refined *version* of reality. The rhetoric of 'reality' is invoked and manipulated to justify another representation, the object of which is in this case the body of a lower-class female. A discourse of contraints, of 'respectability', *enables* a representation, encoding a particular ideological perspective, in the text of Griffin no less, according to his assertion, than in the works of Alma Tadema or Lord Leighton.

Maria Wyke, in analysing reading practices that seek to look 'through' the texts of elegy to a 'reality' of what she terms 'flesh-and-blood' women, also locates herself within the discourse of representation. Again, the relational structure of the term 'representation' defines the problematic, 'a need to determine the relation between the realities of women's lives and their representation in literature'.[9] Granting that the poetic technique of elegy tempts its readers to suppose that to some degree its female subjects reflect the lives of specific Augustan women (and thus suggesting that poetic technique and reading practice have colluded to produce a congruence of past and contemporary perspectives), she argues that 'realism itself is a quality of the text, not a direct manifestation of a "real" world', and that 'to create the aesthetic effect of an open window onto a "reality" lying just beyond, literary works employ a number of formal strategies that change through time and between discourses'.[10] Thus Cynthia's reproaches in Prop. 4.7 are 'replete with apparently authenticating incidentals such as a busy red light district of Rome, worn-down windows, warming cloaks, branded slaves, ex-prostitutes, and wool work'.[11] Sensitive to the way that the strategies of realism and the invocation of that term render the rhetoric of 'reality' problematic, she nonetheless acknowledges the legitimizing power of the term as she warns that 'the realist devices of the Propertian corpus map out only a precarious pathway to the realities of women's lives in Augustan society'.[12] Other pathways are explored only to be rejected, for example finding 'parallel portraits of the female outside the poetic sphere',[13] such as Sallust's Sempronia or Clodia Metelli; but 'these are on the level of representations, not realities – any comparison tends to be a comparison between two forms of discourse about the female'.[14] 'So persuasive have

[9] Wyke (1989a), 25.   [10] Wyke (1989a), 27.   [11] Wyke (1989a), 32.
[12] Wyke (1989a), 33.   [13] Wyke (1989a), 37.   [14] Wyke (1989a), 38.

these discourses on the female been', she continues, 'that they have often been taken for truth.'[15] In the course of her meticulous search, 'representation' has taken over the rhetorical space which 'reality' was presumed to occupy. The 'flesh-and-blood *woman*' produced by one reading practice is significantly replaced by the 'female *form*' of another: the written women of elegy are 'to be read as signifiers of moral and political ideologies'.[16]

The increasing concentration on means rather than object raises a crucial question that can be framed in terms of the 'reality effect': where does it stop? Any assertion that a particular statement in a text represents reality is open to the counter-assertion that it is an instance of the reality effect, that what is *represented* as reality is precisely that, another representation. Within a discourse of representation, increasing formal-ist emphasis on 'means' at the expense of 'object' produces disturbances within the rhetoric of reality and contamination of categories assumed to be discrete: what were assumed to be different turn out to be instances of the same thing, and *vice versa*. The 'conventional devices' which were initially presented as a barrier between 'life' and 'literature' start to take on the role of 'reality'; if the notion of representation is recuperated under these circumstances, it leads to a reversal of categories: 'life' imitates 'literature'. A favourite Ovidian motif, of course,[17] incorporated into the *persona* of the Ovidian lover who, in the received critical tradition, 'takes on the role(s)' of his elegiac predecessors.[18] Griffin presents us ostensibly with a Propertius who models his lover's behaviour on the lifestyle of Antony; but Antony's life*style* turns out to be modelled on the 'role' of the dissolute man of action represented in literature.[19] As the formalist turn is pressed, the opposition between 'life' and 'literature', from which the traditional discourse of representation takes its bearings, starts to fall apart and categories become unstable to the extent of being inverted: 'life' and the practices assumed to constitute it (the musical *fête champêtre*, songs sung outside doors etc) become 'texts', discourses we inhabit; rhetoric is 'reality', *il n'y a pas de hors-texte*, the man is the style, and reality is experienced as a network of representations – seemingly endless, for any representation of reality is open in turn to representation as an instance of the reality effect. However, although the categories have been destabilized, we do not therefore stand outside the discourse of

[15] Wyke (1989a), 40.   [16] Wyke (1989b), 128.
[17] Cf. e.g. *Ars* 2.313, 3.155, 164, 210, *Met*. 11.235–6.
[18] See Davis (1989).   [19] Griffin 1985, 32–47.

representation. The relation of 'standing for' has not been excluded or foreclosed: the discourse of reality becomes the locus for the construction and contestation of ideologies of class, gender and so on; the network of representations now 'stands for' ideological differences. But ideology in turn is not a thing-in-itself: the term 'ideology' is itself precisely determined by the notion of 'perspectival representation' . . . The reader will by now be getting the picture, that 'things' are never *just*, *simply*, *merely* what they seem 'to be', that the 'thing-in-itself', presumed to be an object of representation, becomes in the process itself a representation.

Griffin and Wyke each have their story to tell of Roman love elegy, each producing a textual construct at once itself a representation and itself open to representation. My representation of their texts as 'stories' may seem initially paradoxical, but it does enable further leverage to be exerted on the rhetoric of reality. For in their search for the 'raw stuff of life' and the 'realities of women's lives' at Rome, they invoke the notion of, and inscribe themselves within, a discourse of history, which seeks to ground itself in the actuality of the past; but it is here that the challenge textuality offers to the rhetoric of reality is at its most acute. History constitutes itself as a heuristic discourse by generating, amongst other distinctions, one between the past and the present, the object of history being to recapture the absent past: the past is thus represented as different from the present. But its means of doing so is textual: history fashions *representations* of the past, which create the illusion of reality and make the past 'present'. There is nothing outside the discourses of history by which representations of the past can be checked, no independent access to historical actuality. There is no escape in an appeal to so-called '*Realien*', for they too are open to being represented not as things-in-themselves, as the historicist might wish, but as textually constituted, signifiers never identical with themselves. Hard historicism, which in its purest form would wish to show the past 'as it really was', posits the independent existence of extratextual 'facts', a process of reification rhetorically underpinned by the employment of metaphors that, in speaking of '*hard* facts', '*material* practices', '*flesh-and-blood* women', 'the *raw* stuff of life' and so on, offer immediate and sometimes somewhat sinister sensual gratification. Hard historicism attempts to maintain its position in the face of the textualist emphasis that all 'facts' are discursively constituted as such, all 'events' are always already 'under description' (which is not, incidentally, to deny the actuality of the past but to suggest the process of its discursive organization). In striving to represent the past 'as it really was', to make the past 'present', historicism gestures towards a non-perspectival objectivity despite textualist assertions that history's characterizing structure is teleological,[20] that events are discursively selected, shaped and organized 'under the shadow of the end',[21] that, far from being disinterested, history does precisely make the past 'present' in the sense of accommodating the past to present interests. At its most occlusive, historicism creates 'objective' representations of the past that in their 'immediacy', 'relevance' or 'presence' serve to throw back consoling or affirming self-images; but as textualism encroaches, the distinction between past and present becomes less clearly demarcated, and depictions of the past become more overtly representative of the present. If historicism achieved its aim of understanding a culture of the past 'in its own terms', the result would be totally unintelligible except to but that culture and moment. And arguably not even to that, for a culture is articulated at any point by the contested historicity of its constitutive terms. Far from past being made 'present', it would be rendered totally foreign and impenetrably alien.[22] History cannot present the past in its own terms; it must act to some extent as a translator, an interpreter. The past, even if ostensibly represented as 'different', must also at some level be represented as the 'same'.

History is inextricably locked into the projection, under one guise or another, of 'extratextual realities', and as hard historicism is obliged to soften under the pressure of textualist awareness and critiques, the practice of history reforms itself. As its 'facts' are acknowledged to be textually constituted and its representational devices and modes become visible as such, so rhetorically it creates fresh reifications whose textuality is not immediately apparent, as in 'ideologies'. Realist modes of representation are jettisoned in favour of experimental styles, whilst realism migrates so as to inform other discourses such as sociology or anthropology (or to blur the barriers between them, creating a mixing of genres)[23] – until the next textualist challenge comes along.

The issue of limit and control now becomes pressing, for the anxiety that formalist or textualist approaches raise most starkly is: at what point are such analyses to be *stopped*? At what point *will* they be stopped, since they *can* (apparently) be pressed to the point where categories collapse into an undifferentiated textuality? There lies, we are told, silence or

---

[20] See Attridge, Bennington and Young (1987), 9.
[21] Kermode (1966), 5.   [22] See Felperin (1990), 14.
[23] See chs 2, 4 and 5 below on the work of Halperin, Winkler and Veyne respectively.

madness. Every discursive intervention (including the Nietzschean) attempts or effects a closure of a sort with greater or lesser success, figured in the (illusion of) fulfilment of the desire which informs the intervention. Pygmalion creates a statue; the story 'ends' with it becoming a 'real' woman. However, a sign 'stands' not for reality, but for another sign in a continuing chain of signification. A statue stands for the female body, but the female body is a signifier in its turn; and so on. It is the function and effect of rhetoric to efface itself, to dissolve the distinction between 'illusion' and 'reality' (*ars adeo latet arte sua*). The object of such rhetorical persuasion may be its exponent no less than its audience. Pygmalion's statute 'becomes' a 'real' woman; her 'reality' is beyond question because she 'represents' nothing beyond the fulfilment of his desire. If the female body is the 'object' of representation in Griffin's text, the female form proves too large for the end he wishes to impose. The capacity of signifiers to signify sooner or later evades our control, except in our fantasies; but our sense of control is created *in* our stories, *in* our pictures, *in* our representations. But it is always open to others to tell their stories in their way. Beyond the ostensible *object* of representation, reality as represented by Maria Wyke becomes the locus for the construction and contestation of ideologies of class, gender etc. She seeks in 'ideology' a closural term, but it provides not the destination that the rhetoric promises, but only another resting-place. Closure is provisionally imposed, and the term 'reality' comes into play, when we assert that something stands only for itself, seemingly circumscribed and reflecting our will to control, when the application of a term is deemed a sufficient description, when the verb 'to be' is invoked, an identity asserted, and we say that something *is* something, the 'be-all and end-all'. But just as it looks as though history is set to collapse into an undifferentiated textuality, it comes back with a vengeance and issues its own challenge, that the term 'textuality' itself has a history, that it organizes its discourse teleologically to celebrate its own triumph, that it 'proves' its case by writing . . . history. Just as history 'ends up' (that is, finds the closure it requires to remain usefully operative) talking textuality, so textuality 'ends up' talking history, though always striving to retain the guise of one or the other. Sooner or later (the issue may be represented as one of *deferral*), the contradictions within a term become disablingly obtrusive and can only be resolved by recourse to an appeal to another term to which the first is ostensibly opposed.[24] Thus

---

[24] See ch. 5 below on 'history' and 'aesthetics' in the work of Veyne.

'difference' at some level invokes 'sameness' (recall the musical *fête champêtre* and the plebeian picnic), and *vice versa*. The purest of 'textualizing' definitions of history, 'a kind of storytelling towards the present, a textual construct at once itself, an interpretation and itself open to interpretation',[25] turns out on further inspection to be the most historicizing as well. For to define, to set within limits, to impose closure, to inscribe in a teleological framework, is to historicize.

Textualism allowed to run loose, we are assured, turns all distinctions into undifferentiated textuality, even the reification by which textuality is congealed into texts. Historicism allowed to run loose renders unintelligible even the historical moment it seeks to represent. If the impossible were to happen, if either were to be brought to its 'logical' conclusion (and this can be represented as a possibility only insofar as the terms are projected as extratextual realities), meaning would indeed cease: a text could never reach either horizon without there being total noise or total silence. But the horizon constantly recedes as one approaches, and we are left circumnavigating another hermeneutical circle. Invoking the word 'indeterminacy' is a fine way of making the flesh creep, or creating a warm glow; but its utterance as a meaningful term should offer immediate reassurance, or disappointment, that we haven't got to that stage, and won't, so long as it can create those effects. So, we are not faced with a choice – textuality *or* history – but must live with them both, for it is only in the making and manipulation of such distinctions that meanings can be generated – to the extent to which, in what ways, and to what ends, such terms are kept distinct. Distinctions are often represented as *determining*, but they can also be represented as *enabling*.

There can, then, be no representation without accommodation, no interpretation without appropriation; but equally, there can be no appropriation without interpretation, no accommodation without representation. Any reading, any act of interpretation of a text (of whatever description), is analysable in terms of on the one hand a hermeneutics, which seeks out an originary meaning for a text, and on the other the appropriation of the text by, and its accommodation to, the matrix of practices and beliefs out of which the reading is produced, including the role of the text in the authorization of those beliefs and practices which inform the reading. In establishing its desired goal, the closure to which it is ideally directed, an interpretation sets up a series of distinctions which characteristically incorporate a hierarchy of value, according privilege to one term at the expense of the other in furtherance of the ostensible end. A historicizing hermeneutical approach works to open up a distinction between text and context, projecting the second as ancillary to the first. The tendency of this is to locate the meaning of a text in the original moment of inscription and to represent all previous contextualizations as detachable, closed 'episodes' in the text's *Nachleben*, thus projecting the present contextualization as the 'truth', the 'real meaning'. A discourse of appropriation works to blur any distinction between text and context in its emphasis on the contextual construction of textual meaning – that every context is precisely another text, a construction open to interpretation – and stresses the multiplicity of contexts. But although this approach emphasizes that all readings are equally rhetorical, it baulks at the suggestion that all readings are therefore equally true; an agenda is no less at work here, leading to its own *telos*. The 'most plausible' or 'best' reading from this perspective is that which sees in the text the closest figuration of present preoccupations, and previous contextualizations are retrospectively seen as accommodated to the preoccupations of their periods – now treated by the imposition of closure as 'episodes', their awkward openness now (apparently) safely under control. The more strongly the figuration is felt, the more emphatic the assertion that it is objectively 'there' in the text, and has been 'present' in it all along, albeit locally suppressed and awaiting recovery. By contrast, a 'historicizing' rhetoric will tend to occlude notions of appropriation.[26] But however much an approach succeeds in marginalizing one term at the expense of the other, the other always remains operative within it, however occluded, and renders the reading available for recuperation for and in the very terms occluded. Allowing the occluded terms to bounce back relativizes the findings (not necessarily refuting them – for all findings depend on distinctions being operative and are validated or negated only within the terms of the discourse which produces them – but rendering them open to recontextualization); reveals the pretensions of the previous reading, its claims to authority as presenting the 'truth'; and exposes the provisionality of closures represented as final, opening up the discourse to further acts of interpretation.

The issue of how far one term is going to be pressed at the expense of the other constitutes the politics of interpretation, that is, the discourse

---

[26] See ch. 5 below.

representing positionality 'inside' and 'outside' the formation of scholarship. Thus to represent recent criticism of Roman love elegy as historicizing emerges as a truism (for how could it fail to be so in some fashion?) and as a claim to a position within the scholarly formation. What is represented as 'historicism' (or 'textualism') is never *simply* an example of historicism or textualism (since one incorporates the other at some level), but also includes the perspectival positionality of the term's use, in the continuing (but not *end*less) contestation over what are to be projected as the 'norms' of interpretation – a struggle in which one's own approach will be represented as 'truths to be defended' and 'firmly-grounded methodologies' and one's opponent's as 'ideologies to be uncovered' and strategies of evasion, domestication, recuperation, accommodation and so on.

A 'reading' is not a closed system, identical with itself, however much it seeks to impose, or succeeds in imposing, closure on the chain of representations. It is always more or less accommodated to the context in which it appears, and for which it has been invoked, ordered and shaped, as is clearly the case with my readings of Griffin and Wyke no less than of the Pygmalion story in Ovid or the Tibullan readings to follow, which make 'Griffin', 'Wyke', 'Ovid' and 'Tibullus' *representative* of particular perspectives. A reading is thus, beyond its ostensible function as *explication du texte*, an allegory of itself and a justification of its own procedures, constitutive of the discourse of representation which seeks to represent it. If the Pygmalion story 'responds' to a discourse of representation, it can hardly do otherwise when it is re-constituted as a projection of it. Attempts to formalize, to systematize, run up against this problem sooner or later. It can only be deferred, so long as *a* reading can be made to appear *the* meaning of a text.

Any text, be it a Roman elegy or this one, must present itself at some level as having a 'universal' or transhistorical aspect even as it addresses a specific moment, if it is to be interpreted at all. What Thucydides presents as polar opposites (1.22), works written *es to parachrēma* rather than designed to stand as a *ktēma es aiei* (but then, as a self-styled historicist he has an interest in opening up this distinction, just as a self-styled textualist has an interest in closing it), are of necessity ingredients of any intelligible text. The universality occurs when a text projects, or is interpreted as projecting, a term as of universal validity or applicability, identical with itself, an essentialism – a theme I will be considering in greater depth in chapter 2 in relation to the terms love, sex and gender. In order to depict and argue for the multiplicity of representations, it is necessary to project 'representation' as a foundational term of transhistorical validity, a preoccupation 'present' in the texts of the past; in order to argue for 'differences' it is necessary to posit sameness or identity, and *vice versa*. A discourse of 'representation' provides a set of terms which enable and determine the articulation of issues of reality, identity, control etc. With all this in mind, let us examine some texts of elegy from the (inevitably restricted) viewpoint (sic) of representation.

A prominent place has been given in recent critical writing to elegies which concentrate realist devices within the framework of a narrative description delivered in the first person and identified with the author, to the extent that this mode is projected as representative of elegy as a whole; Propertius 1.3, 2.15, 4.8 and Ovid, *Amores* 1.5 are repeatedly adduced as the classic examples. This does scant justice, it should be said, to the variety of representational strategies explored in the genre. One might adduce, for example, the contrasting narrators and expository styles of Book 4 of Propertius,[27] the use of a mythical female narrator within an epistolary framework in Ovid's *Heroides*, or the contrasting perspectives offered by the male friend of Sulpicia and by Sulpicia of Sulpicia's relationship with Cerinthus in [Tib.] 4.2–6 and 7–12 respectively. One of the most sustained, searching and sophisticated experiments in representational strategy is formed by the Delia poems of Tibullus (1.1–3, 5 and 6). This cycle can be read in such a way as to render problematic precisely what is 'taken for granted' in readings of elegy, the first-person male authorial *persona*. These poems have often been dismissed as disorganized concatenations of motifs, and, although this is a view which has become increasingly difficult to defend,[28] they are tantalizingly elusive. The first poem seems to be a monologue of some sort, representing the words or thoughts of what for the moment I shall refer to as its 'speaker'. The opening lines express a willingness that others may face the hardships and dangers of war abroad in pursuit of great wealth in contrast to the speaker's wish for a life of inglorious inactivity at home (1–6). But who is this speaker? His identity is available to us only through his words, and thus far we have heard only the expression of desire via a series of subjunctive verbs. The circumstances, the 'facts', the 'realities' which have prompted the expression of these desires, or are preventing their fulfilment, have not yet been divulged and

---

[27] See Wyke (1987b). [28] See Cairns (1979), 192.

will only emerge in the speaker's words. But for the moment, the subjunctives continue. As a *rusticus*, a peasant (7–8), he would set vines with expertise, nor would his hopes play him false, but deliver a bumper vintage. His words have not made clear whether he does, or does not, regard himself as a *rusticus*, and, if so, what is standing in the way of him accomplishing what he wishes, but his wishes for a bumper vintage are characterized by an undoubted confidence in their fulfilment, for he says, employing an indicative at last in his first explicit self-characterization, that he *is* a man of piety (*veneror*, 'I pay homage', 11), and his further description of the piety he represents as characteristic of himself reveals through another indicative (*ponitur*, 14) that he *is* a country property-owner of some sort ('and a portion of whatever fruit the new harvest brings forth for me *is* placed before the farmer god', 13–14). The speaker's 'real' circumstances are emerging in his words. What, then, is preventing the fulfilment of his wishes of 5–8, and of the promises he subsequently makes to honour Ceres, the goddess who would guarantee such fruitfulness, and Priapus, the god who would guard it (15–18)? The address in the indicative to the Lares that follows (19–22) reveals in passing another important circumstantial detail, that the speaker's property, which was once huge, is now greatly reduced. The optative subjunctives that resume in 25–6,

> iam modo, iam possim contentus vivere parvo
> nec semper longae deditus esse viae . . .

if only now, now at last, I may be able to live content with little,
and not always be given up to the long march . . .

reveal obliquely the reason why the speaker is unable to tend his reduced estate: 'if only I may not always be given up to the long march' implies that that is precisely what he is, a soldier duty-bound to serve far from home. His reasons for becoming a soldier are not made explicit, but his opening expression of willingness that others should go away to war in pursuit of wealth so long as he might be able to stay at home in his reduced circumstances can be read retrospectively in this light. Similarly, the serving soldier's reverie about making love to a mistress on the familiar couch at home while the storm rages outside (43–50) turns out in retrospect to have been prompted in relation to a specific individual, *mea Delia* (57), and the elaborate series of plays throughout the text on words applicable to both warfare and love-making[29] can be seen as 'generated'

---

[29] See Lee (1974).

out of the solider/lover's 'experience' and articulating the ironies and conflict of values involved in his situation.

The text is thus, obliquely, providing its own context, a 'reality' notionally 'outside' it against which the speaker's identity can be constructed, his character delineated and his perspectives assessed, and it is possible to construct a very detailed 'context' (as for example Cairns does for 1.5, setting out in tabular form the '"historical" order' of events and their 'actual order of presentation'[30]), and to explore the ramifying discrepancies and resonances between the text and its 'context'. The addresses to Messalla (53ff.) and Delia (57ff.) suggest a dramatic aspect to the monologue, but if the 'setting' is, as lines 25–6 seem to imply, abroad on military service, the possibility that both of them are envisaged as present to hear it seems to be excluded, leaving it probable that neither is to be thought of as listening. Rather the implication is that the text represents the sequence of the 'speaker's' thought, and that we read it as eavesdroppers on a stream of consciousness, thus involving us in the piquant circularity of extrapolating 'reality' from the text and then using it to assess the viewpoint from which that 'reality' has been presented. The address to Messalla serves, apparently, to anchor the text's ostensible context in turn in specific historical 'reality', whether we wish to represent that as the undoubted physical existence of Messalla, or the ideological values he is represented as embodying so successfully (53–4).

However, the Delia cycle does not fold itself unproblematically into that specific historical 'reality'. 1.3 projects its 'setting' as the soldier/lover falling ill on the way to the campaign with Messalla and in danger of dying. Again the addresses to both Messalla (1f.) and Delia (82ff.), who is repeatedly represented as having been left behind, suggest that we are eavesdropping on a monologue in the mind. The soldier/lover has fallen ill on the island of 'Phaeacia' (3). There were a number of contemporary discourses which sought to identify the Homeric Phaeacia with the island of Corcyra,[31] but contextualizations which seek to ground themselves in the 'realities' of the poet's biography or the immediate circumstances of composition and substitute 'Corcyra' for 'Phaeacia', often without comment, thereby sidestep the very issue of the distinction between 'truth' and 'fiction', the 'real' and the 'fictive' which the name 'Phaeacia' problematizes. It will not do to seek a final meaning in the signifier 'Tibullus', for what is signified by 'Tibullus' is one of the points at issue. We eavesdrop on the thoughts of 'Tibullus' as he believes he is

---

[30] Cairns (1979), 176–8.   [31] See Cairns (1979), 44–6.

about to die. He reviews what happened between him and Delia immediately before his departure from that perspective – under the shadow of the end, we might say – (9–22), revealing the way his representation of the past is structured around his present concerns, and his interpretations of the 'same' event fluctuate through changing circumstances. Immediately before his departure, Delia, he recalls, is said (*dicitur*, 10) to have consulted all the gods about his prospects of return; *dicitur* implies he was not present and knew this only by report. All the omens (*par excellence* a discourse of signs whose interpretation is contingent upon circumstance) promised his safe return (13), although Delia's behaviour gave every indication that she was not convinced by them. At that juncture his casual attitude to the omens (sought by Delia and not by him) was determined by the desire to use them, and Delia's reaction to them, in order to cast himself in the role of *solator* (15), a comforter, and, after the last farewell, separated from Delia, to seek in them a (now anxious) excuse for not going just yet (15–16). Following his departure, which involved a stumble in the gateway (20), changing circumstances lead him increasingly (cf. *quotiens*, 19) to brood upon these signs and to deem them unlucky (*tristia*, 20), a chain of interpretation seemingly validated by his present plight. His self-identification as a lover within this monologue provides the explanation and the moral to be drawn: let no-one dare to depart from a lover who doesn't wish it, or he will know that he has gone against the prohibition of the god (21–2). The implied circumstances and self-image of the lover determine the details of the escapist fantasy of a Golden Age in the past, when there were no long roads for marches (*longas . . . vias*, 36), no ships to take men overseas in search of wealth, no warfare, no doors to houses (37–48). This is similarly the case when he seeks refuge from his helplessness in weaving elaborate fantasies about a heaven for those who have died young in love (57–66) and a hell for anyone who would wish to desecrate not, as it transpires, love in general, but his own affair (67–82), this last fading into an Odyssean fantasy of the welcome he might receive from Delia should he return safely (83–92).

What emerges from this ostensibly private stream of consciousness upon which we eavesdrop is a complex mixture of fantasy and oblique narrative emplotted from the perspective of one whose circumstance is impending death and whose self-image is overwhelmingly that of a lover. Nonetheless, at one point this monologue contemplates projecting out into the 'world' a 'text' which offers a quite different perspective. Fearful of the imminence of death, the lover composes his epitaph, which will be open to 'public' scrutiny in a way that his 'thoughts' will not be:

> hic iacet immiti consumptus morte Tibullus
> Messallam terra dum sequiturque mari   (55–6)

Here lies Tibullus taken off by a cruel death while serving with Messalla on land and sea

For 'public' consumption, the lover who imagines himself cavorting around the Elysian Fields or returning to the arms of his rapturous beloved, wishes to be seen (fantasizes being seen?) as the model of a loyal soldier, following his commander even to his death. Giving to the lover/soldier the name 'Tibullus' further complicates the issue. Which constitutes the 'real' identity, the lover or the soldier (or the person his friends 'know' as 'the poet'; compare the contrasting representations in Horace, *Odes* 1.33 and *Epistles* 1.4)? Or does the 'real' identity lie in the incongruity and conflict between the roles? From where does the definition of our identity arise? From the interpretations by others of our actions and words? In the face of the entanglement in (oftentimes bewildering, dangerous or distasteful) circumstance which the social pressures on the construction of our identities exert, fantasy seems to offer a reassuring sense of control by allowing desire untrammelled freedom. However, fantasy is not separate from reality but helps to constitute it, and only becomes perceived as separate and open to representation as 'fantasy' when the closure it seeks to impose is superseded and becomes untenable. In 1.5, the setting for which is the street outside Delia's door up and down which he walks, the locked-out lover recalls how he used to fashion a future for himself and Delia (21–34), an idyllic existence in the country in which Delia would grow accustomed to rural life, to the extent that she could take over the running of everything (29–30), and be the perfect hostess to Messalla on his visits (31–4). *consuescet* (25) tempts one to extrapolate about the 'reality' of Delia's character which the lover's fantasy was at that stage striving to override. Changed perception (which now appropriates for itself the role of 'reality') has rendered this picture untenable, a 'fantasy'; the verbatim recollection is framed between two uses of the verb *fingebam*, 'I used to imagine' (20, 35), and to the first of these the lover appends from his present perspective the adjective *demens*, representing himself from the perspective of now as 'out of his mind' then – precisely when, it could be argued, he was most *in* it. The dominant theme of the Delia cycle on this reading is *real*ization, the rendering of 'reality' to oneself.

It is high time, however, that some pressure were exerted on the rhetoric of this form of analysis, the way the argument has been structured to suggest that 'in reality' these poems are monologues, that the text generates within itself a context against which it might be read and so forth. This can be done by looking at another of the Delia poems which can be interpreted in such a way as to render visible some of the rhetorical strategies involved in this reading. The poems thus far examined have been read as projecting as their 'setting' a particular moment and place from which the lover emplots the events of the past and projects his vision of the future. 1.2 has placed considerable difficulties in the path of a similar analysis. Guy Lee has summarized the problem well:

> This long elegy appears to have a dramatic setting, but readers differ over what that setting is. Some think the whole thing takes place at Delia's closed door (the wine referred to in line 1 could be served there, cf. Plautus *Curculio* 82–85). Others think that it takes place at a drinking-party, at which the poet from line 7 on falls into a reverie, possibly (as Leo suggested) coming out of it at line 89 when someone present laughs. Still others think that the poet is at home, soliloquizing after initially addressing a servant; a variant of this would be that he falls asleep after line 6 and what follows represents his thoughts in a vivid dream.[32]

Let us take a hint from Lee's use of the phrase 'dramatic setting' and explore the poem as the projection of, and response to, not one particular moment and place but a developing series of situations which the lover both responds to and prompts – a fully-fledged dramatic monologue, that is. His opening words represent him as trying to get drunk in response to *novos . . . dolores*, new miseries (1), the adjective implying perhaps that this is not the first time things have gone wrong. He finds himself outside his girl's firmly bolted door (5–6), to which he addresses a typical lover's lament (7–14): where elsewhere the lover's words were addressed only to himself, in his mind, his lament we may imagine him as uttering aloud. His initial curse directed at the door on finding it locked

---

[32] Lee (1990), 116. I have used Lee's text and enumeration in the following discussion.

(7–8) turns immediately into an obsequious apology to it (9–12), and then, in the hope that it may yet open to let him in, into a reminder of the many times he has decorated it with garlands – frequently the action of a lover who has had to depart unsuccessfully,[33] and so an oblique confirmation of the situation adumbrated in the phrase *novos . . . dolores* (1). Delia is then addressed through the door (15–24). She may have another man or she may be under guard to prevent her meeting the lover; he assumes the alternative that offers him greater hope, and addresses encouragement to her which articulates his image of her desired behaviour: the goddess of love favours lovers who show courage in overcoming the obstacles to furtive love-making, but not to everyone, only those whom 'fear does not stop getting up in the dark of the night' (*quos . . . nec vetat obscura surgere nocte timor*, 23–4). *en* (25) usually draws attention to action happening at the precise moment of its utterance, and *ego cum tenebris tota vagor anxius urbe* ('when I wander distraught throughout the city in the dark'), uttered from the lover's perspective as demonstrative proof that Venus protects brave lovers, seems to indicate as well that he has now left the doorstep; his point of departure may be signalled in *surgere* (24), for the action signified there could instigate his departure from the door just as much as describe the behaviour desired of Delia. Venus renders courageous lovers inviolable, the lover tells himself (29–30), as he catalogues the possible dangers faced by a lover wandering the streets alone at night, the first which occurs to him being assault and theft (27–8). But whether it be the dangers of mugging or the frost and rain, any hardship, he tells himself, is worthwhile if only Delia will invite him in (33–4). The startled exclamation *parcite luminibus* (35; eyes or torches?), presumably prompted by his first encounter with another person, seems to give the lie to the lover's much-vaunted courage. His following words combine an attempt to recuperate that self-image with a warning to anyone who might recognize him to keep his mouth shut, implying that recognition *as* a lover is chief amongst his anxieties (37–42). Not that Delia's *coniunx* will believe an informer anyway, he tells himself (43; the reason for the lover's earlier exclusion is becoming clearer with the lover's explicit allusion to this character *as* Delia's *coniunx*, her partner), since the lover has obtained a spell from a witch so that he won't believe his eyes, even if he catches the lover and Delia in bed together (55–8); but the lover's

---

[33] See Smith (1913), 210, ad loc.

anxieties about Delia's attachment to him emerge as he adds that the spell will only work for him, not for other potential or actual lovers (59–60). His faith in the witch seems total as he recalls to himself the demonstration of her powers that he witnessed (45–54), but on further reflection (61–6) his faith rapidly evaporates, as he recalls that the witch promised to free him from his love and carried out ceremonies to do so. But her failure is hardly surprising, since it immediately transpires that while all this was going on, the lover himself was praying (cf. *orabam*, 66) not that his love should go away, but that it should be mutual, and that he shouldn't be able to live without Delia.

The lover's capacity for self-delusion seems boundless, as every successive utterance works to undermine the realities he has previously unfolded for himself. Another figure now enters his thoughts, an iron-hearted man who, when he had Delia for the asking, preferred, the fool (*stultus*, 68), to go abroad to war in the successful pursuit of plunder and glory (67–72). The lover contrasts his aspirations starkly with those of the soldier, if only *he* had the opportunity to be with Delia (*mea si tecum modo Delia*, 73), and they are his characterizing dream of life and love in the country (73–6). What, he asks himself, is the point of luxurious bedding, feather pillows and the soothing sound of running water, if you spend the night awake crying (77–80)? The iron-hearted man is not explicitly identified, but the account of his activities in 67–70 has a ring of familiarity, and the details of the remorse attributed to him in 77–80 are remarkably specific. Can it be that this is the lover's *alter ego*, whose behaviour is now so unaccountable to him that he can only refer to it as though it were that of another person entirely? The account of the luxurious bedding in 77 arises out of, and in contrast to, the lover's dream of making love to Delia in the country, and his assertion that *his* sleep (cf. *mihi*) would be *mollis*, soft, on the uncultivated ground (76). The adjective carries the connotation that this would be the sleep that follows on love-making.[34] We only ever 'see' Delia through the words of the lover, and must construct our image of what she is 'really' like from the perspectives these offer; but from his previous references to *molli . . . lecto* (19) and *molli . . . toro* (58), in both of which the figure of Delia is implicated, it is at least open to us to wonder what her reaction to the prospect of making love on the uncultivated ground might be, let alone her attitude to a lover who went away to war to enrich himself when he

[34] See Cairns (1979), 102.

could have had her for the asking. The lover turns to wondering whether his present predicament could be the result of displeasing the goddess of love (81–4); if so, he wouldn't hesitate to crawl on his hands and knees and beat his head against the door of her temple (85–8). At this point he addresses a warning: 'but you who complacently laugh at my woes, beware; your turn will come' (89–90). Presumably his attention has been caught by the sound of laughter and he realizes that he is the object of it. What dramatically will have prompted the laughter? What, indeed, prompted the thought in 81ff. that he might have displeased Venus? Is it that on his nocturnal ramblings he has arrived at the temple of Venus, and is carrying out the actions he refers to as his penance? It is to address her that he turns once more (99–100) when he has delivered his warning to the person who derided him (91–8).

Doubtless this reading could be altered, supplemented or challenged; it presents itself as one more or less plausible 'contextualization' of the text. But to what extent is it 'outside' the text, as the term 'contextualization' seems to suggest? We have already seen the way the other Delia poems 'invade' their possible contextualizations in such a way as to blur the distinction between text and context. Lee's use of the term 'dramatic setting'[35] can be developed to produce a reading of the poem as the representation of action, the subject-matter and rapid changes of scene being reminiscent of mime, a genre with which elegy has a number of affinities.[36] Possibly Tibullus 1.2 was amenable to some form of dramatic performance, as Virgil's *Eclogues* reportedly were. That is an intriguing possibility, but neither its establishment nor its refutation would 'fix' or guarantee the meaning of the text. The notion of 'performance' entailed by and encoded in a phrase like 'dramatic setting' can serve a variety of rhetorical functions, and its attendant terminology is available for appropriation in various ways to underpin differing types of interpretation with differing interests. From one perspective, performance is 'outside' the text, an interpretation of it: the term 'performance' enacts a distinction between a 'transcendent' text and the specific, imperfect *interpretations, embodiments, representations, realizations* of it. But from another perspective, performance of a text is the means of self-exploration or self-expression on the part of the performers.[37] This

[35] Comparable terms are found elsewhere of this poem; e.g. Smith speaks of its 'mise-en-scène' (1913, 45).   [36] See McKeown (1979).

[37] See Sayre (1990); also ch. 4 below on the representation of the lover's discourse as 'script'.

perspective informs, for example, criticism of drama which seeks the 'meaning' of a play not in the 'transcendent text', but in its specific performances, seen, say, as ritual or the enactment of civic ideology. This sort of criticism seeks a closure in the representation of drama as an *embodiment*, the material 'presence' of the body being seen as the guarantor of meaning. But the closure is a provisional one, for the body is not a self-evident 'reality' signifying nothing beyond itself, and perform-ance in this scheme is itself an enactment of something further (religious belief or civic ideology), and thus itself a 'text' to be interpreted. As a text 'dramatizes' action, it becomes part of this chain of signification, and we discover ourselves in a delightful world of ironic resonances in which the 'reality' of one text dramatizing action finds rhetorical corroboration in the 'realism' of another, as when Margaret Hubbard says of Propertius 4.8: 'we could not be ... more firmly located in the *verismo* of the mime'.[38] Within this chain of representations, all the world's a stage, and the discourses we inhabit are 'scripts' so 'real' to those involved that they 'act' upon them. One cannot impose a closure on Tibullus 1.2 by referring to the person Tibullus, for 'Tibullus' is an exploration of the roles, poetic and erotic, the elegy dramatizes. Elegy's place in this chain of significa-tion is encoded in Ovid's warning to the censorious at the beginning of the second book of the *Amores* (2.1.3–4):

> procul hinc, procul este, severi:
> non estis teneris apta *theatra* modis

> Away with you from here, those of you with puritan views: you
> are not a fit *audience* for erotic strains

A text (of whatever description) cannot seal itself off from, it can only occlude its own involvement in, the terms of analysis it seeks to impose. In ostensibly talking *about* representation and the terminology it involves, I have not been able to escape using it myself; the opening sentence of this chapter read 'the notion of representation *plays a prominent role* in aesthetic criticism', and the language of 'seeing' (perspective, viewpoint, ostensibly, etc.) pervades it. It is possible to articulate only within the terms of a discourse, but if this is determining from one perspective, it can also be represented as enabling. One can devise strategies of provisional evasion, such as I have done in talking about the '*discourse* of representation' which projects a position 'outside'

[38] Hubbard (1974), 151.

from which the illusion of control can be created and suggests that certain terms 'within' it (notably 'representation') are foundational and not problematic, and in manipulating terminology (e.g. 'closure') in such a way as to suggest it lies beyond sceptical scrutiny. The distinctions imposed in any discourse are always arbitrary in the sense that they cannot be grounded in any appeal to something 'outside' the discourse, but never arbitrary in the sense that the distinctions are discursively produced. In criticizing the 'rhetoric' of reality (that is, the way *others* use the term), one cannot avoid creating a 'reality' within which one's own discourse is ostensibly grounded. The reader may care to look again at the indicative statements in this chapter. It is salutary to see in every 'answer' another question, in every 'disavowal of authority' the construction of another 'authority', to regard the time one thinks one is right as the time to think again. Indicative statements; but indicative of what?

Getting down to essentials

From the perspectives offered by modern criticism, the elegies of
Tibullus, Propertius and Ovid are 'about' a wide variety of issues –
politics, patronage, their own status vis-à-vis other genres, for example –
but they seek their ultimate definition as the poetry of *amor*. Ovid's first
collection of elegies is called *Amores*, a title which recalls that apparently
given to his four books of elegies by Cornelius Gallus, thus giving rise
from the very beginning to the assumption that their subject will be *amor*;
and on virtually any account *amor* is indeed central to elegiac discourse.
But what does it *mean*? Such a question seeks its answer in an
essentializing definition. The assumption that the word primarily or
exclusively stands for or refers to the experience of an emotion informs
most standard treatments of elegy: these poems are ultimately 'about' the
love of Propertius for Cynthia or Ovid for Corinna. But if *amor* can
signify an emotion, it can also, as we've already seen, signify the title of a
book. In poem 1.7 of Propertius, which is addressed to a person called
Ponticus who is described as an epic poet writing a work that will rival
those of Homer, the speaker says of himself in contrast (5), *nos, ut
consuemus, nostros agitamus amores*: I, as I have been accustomed to do,
get on with my – *amores*. Does this mean a love affair or writing love
poetry? Or both? This is only to start to explore the possibilities of
meaning of the word *amor*, the chain of signification that will be a
recurrent theme of the coming chapters. The opening of Book 2 of Ovid's
Ars amatoria has a nice image for this. There *Amor* is Cupid, the boy with
wings, and the poet remarks how difficult it is to impose a limit on them
(*difficile est illis inposuisse modum*, 20), an apt image for a signifier with a
mobile meaning and a constantly shifting area of reference that is
potentially as broad as the world itself (cf. *tam vasto pervagus orbe puer*,

18). You may think you have imposed a definition on the word only to find it taking wing once more and then settling, temporarily, in another area of experience previously assumed to be discrete.

One cannot evade the issue of *meaning* by an appeal to the multiplicity of meanings, however. To render *amor* as 'love', dictionary-fashion, supplies a meaning, but suppresses the process by which words acquire *meaning* and significance in use, and language moulds its meanings in relation to different discursive situations. The production of meaning is a social phenomenon; the meanings of words are affirmed and challenged in every utterance, and this process of contestation is itself part of the meaning of language-in-use. To the question *what* does *amor* mean, which invites the closure of an essentializing definition, must always be added the question *how* does it mean? Interpretation can be represented in terms of translatability. At one extreme, which enacts a very violent disjunction between word and context, there is the substitution of a term in one language ('love') deemed the 'equivalent' of a term in another (*amor*). The Western tradition is founded upon the belief, or it may be faith, in the translatability of such terms, that when a Roman author writes *amor*, even if we use a different word, we in some way know what is meant. But translatability is an issue not only *between* languages but *within* a language as well. Can the word *amor* (or, as it may be, 'love') ever mean exactly the same to two people given their inevitably different perspectives? The issue of translatability taken down to this level generates the search for (or the desire to impose) mutuality, communality of meaning, in the use of the term 'love', which constitutes the lover's discourse.[1] The meaning proposed for a word and the context in which it is invoked are here inseparably entwined; quite the opposite of being seen as universally valid, terms from this perspective become essentially contested. As a corollary to this, will a word mean the same to the same person (even the author of a text) in two different situations, on two different readings? To be readable at all, even to its author, a text, even as it addresses a specific moment, or defines its terms as (culturally) specific, must project terms within it as of transhistorical validity to a greater or lesser degree. The conditions which enable the composition of the text in the first place then render it available for translation, both within the culture which produced it and between cultures, permitting the mapping on to the text of, and the simultaneous appropriation of the text to

---

[1] This theme will be resumed in ch. 4 below.

underpin, the concerns which inform the reading. These concerns will, in turn, already have been moulded by previous appropriations of the text. Thus elegy essentializes *amor* as its master term and projects it into the successive appropriations of the texts which constitute the discourse of Roman *love* elegy.

The recent 'turn' towards textuality has brought fresh awareness of the occluded rhetoricity of essentializing terms granted transhistorical validity. The issues involved, particularly the role of essentialism, have been most thoroughly explored within the discourses of gender and sexuality, and the perspectives developed there intersect with and are applicable to the discourse of love in turn. The methodological approaches involved can be most easily illustrated by generating a specific issue. Modern readers of Roman elegy are often struck by what many of them would term its 'homosexual' element. Tibullus has a cycle of three poems in his first book concerning love for the boy Marathus interspersed with those dealing with the girl Delia. Propertius 2.4 contrasts the pain of loving women with the comparative calm of loving boys, whilst in the opening poem of Book 1 of Ovid's *Amores* the poet argues with Cupid that he can't be expected to write elegy because he doesn't have the *materia*, the subject-matter appropriate to the genre, *aut puer aut longas compta puella comas* (19–20), either a boy or a girl with long hair, with the implication that either would be sufficient. This element, and the terms in which it is categorized, are negotiated in various ways. In some cases, there is total silence. Sometimes there is acknowledgement, but it is implicitly downgraded by the argument that the poems of heterosexual love in some way represent the 'reality' of the poets' love lives whereas those concerning boys are 'literary exercises' in imitation of Greek models, or that elsewhere, for example, Ovid expresses a personal preference for heterosexual relationships (*Ars* 2.683–4); and in other cases we are presented with detailed accounts of the social conventions or anatomical particulars of same-sex relationships. All of these responses are, of course, open to representation as ideological perspectives within the continuing contestation over the legitimacy of homosexual desires or practices, but, whilst no statement, or indeed silence, about sex can be value-free or objective, the contemporary discourses of sexuality and gender, themselves of course implicated in this contestation, often in pursuit of very specific stated objectives, should alert us to the pitfalls of appropriatively 'reading off' such perspectives unproblematically, although, in that all interpretation involves appropriation, all reading involves reading off. No account can be so positive as to resist reconfiguration and transformation, even to the extent of reversing the ostensible tenor of the argument.[2]

The characteristic move of these discourses recently has been to emphasize the 'otherness' and the 'specificity' of the past. Thus, for Michel Foucault, the experience of sexuality is not the experience of a natural phenomenon that has always existed, though modern perspectives have often assumed it to be so, but an experience that has a specific, and quite recent, historical genesis. An analysis of what was said about sex in the pagan and early Christian world, he argued, would reveal an 'experience of the flesh'[3] quite different from the modern experience of sexuality. Sexuality, he asserted, has come to be presented in modern Western society as the key which unlocks the door to the hidden, inner essence of a person (as though saying 'so-and-so *is* "bisexual"'' were a sufficient or exhaustive description of him or her), or as a means of self-definition, whereby we have come to feel that it is more important to scrutinize ourselves and establish our own sense of identity in terms of our 'sexuality' rather than, say, our eating habits.[4] What he sees as this modern obsession with sex operates, he argues, in a particular way: namely, as a means to define and categorize people through their 'sexuality'. 'Sexuality' is thus a reality in that it is a phenomenon that is experienced, whether it be in a sense of anxiety over one's sexual identity, or in the social consequences of being labelled, or labelling oneself, as having a particular sexual identity. 'Sexuality' has this role in our thought and experience because it has become the focus for an interplay of knowledge and power. In different historical periods, different kinds of assumptions and methods of argument are accorded validity and are believed to be able to distinguish between truth and falsehood. The central role given to 'sexuality' has developed hand-in-hand with the formation of domains of 'knowledge', such as psychology or the study of sexual behaviour, to whose arguments and findings we attribute validity, truth-value and authority. The use of the seemingly objective criterion of the sex of the object-choice, combined with the passing across what Foucault termed the 'threshold of scientificity'[5] of a psychiatric style of reasoning (with its characteristic criteria, modes of argumentation and explanation which made increasing room for discussions of impulses,

[2] See Halperin (1990), 52.   [3] Foucault (1986a), 339.
[4] Foucault (1986b), 10; 51–2.   [5] Foucault (1972), 190; cf. Davidson (1987/8), 48.

desires and tastes, and allowed theories propounded within it to be deemed 'true' or 'false'[6]), enabled the emergence of a taxonomy, a set of categories which, whatever about 'appearances' (a rhetoric which works to downgrade cultural and environmental considerations), could establish the 'real' identity or nature of an individual. These emergent discourses become viewed as domains of knowledge, normative systems that work to determine the way people experience and to regulate their conduct. From this perspective, then, 'sexuality' and its constituent categories are a comparatively recent phenomenon, as suggested in the polemical title David M. Halperin gave to his collection of essays, *One Hundred Years of Homosexuality*.[7] That is not to say that people did not participate in sexual acts with others of the same sex before this, nor that these practices were any less open to ideological representation than they are nowadays; but such people did not think of themselves, nor were they thought of as, 'homosexuals', and the pattern of ideological representation was accordingly different. As Paul Veyne has remarked, the ancient world did not view the experience of homosexuality as a separate problem.[8] There was neither the term, nor the system of reasoning, the discourses, that would have supported the term. But the ancients did have their own categories and discourses, specific to their own culture, which have been displaced, no less than the dominant contemporary classifications will be.

In developing its critique of related assumptions about sexual identity, gender criticism has used complementary modes of argumentation. Just as in many languages gender is not necessarily correlated with sex, so the choice of 'gender' rather than 'sex' to designate sexual identity and its associated characteristics emphasizes that biological sex does not inevitably generate or determine the characteristics conventionally associated with it. Gender critics suggest that categories and distinctions are produced in discourse which are characterized in terms of the opposition male/female, so that these categories or qualities are seen as 'essentially' masculine or 'essentially' feminine. Wherever there is such a polar opposition, an implicit hierarchy operates which attaches superior value to one pole; thus 'male' is frequently seen as superior and the norm, 'female' as inferior and judged in relation to the male. Such hierarchies are then often underpinned by the enormously powerful discourse of nature: it is a man's *nature* to be, say, aggressive or individualistic, and it

---

[6] See Davidson (1987/8), 22. [7] Halperin (1990).

[8] Veyne (1985), 26; is this to be read as '*separate* problem' or 'separate *problem*'?

is a woman's *nature* to be, say, submissive or self-sacrificing. From this perspective, gender is opposed to sex as culture is to nature, and consequently, sexual identities, however internalized and regarded as 'natural' by those who bear them, are for gender critics culturally specific *roles*, and character traits are not autonomous, immanent qualities but functions and ways of relating. The terms of this debate could be represented as 'already explored' (and 'already deconstructed' if one so wishes) in Ovid's discussion of the roles of the sexes in taking the initiative in sexual encounters (*Ars* 1.277–8): *conveniat maribus ne quam nos ante rogemus | femina iam partes victa rogantis aget* ('were it to be agreed amongst males that we should not take the lead in courtship, the female, overwhelmed by desire, will play that role'); female libido is 'by nature' stronger (Ovid uses female animals by way of 'proof', 279–80), but it is a 'convention' that males, although desire is more moderate and not so vehement amongst 'us' (*parcior in nobis nec tam furiosa libido*, 281), should take the initiative.

Modes of analysis such as these are used to decentre established accounts and to challenge their pretensions to truth. For example, the vocabulary used in Latin to describe people who engage in sexual acts with others of the same sex is full of Greek terms such as *cinaedus*, *pathicus*, *tribas*, although these are not to be found in the elegists. Ramsey MacMullen uses the word 'importation'[9] of this phenomenon and remarks: 'Had open love of male by male been *as much at home* in Rome as in Greece, one would not expect the expression of it to be sought in such derivative terms.'[10] However, controversial sexual matters are often put in foreign terms as a means of negotiating the effects of mentioning them at all; compare the use of the quasi-medical Latin terms *fellatio* and *cunnilingus* in English to refer to oral sex – the decent obscurity of a learned tongue, as it is sometimes referred to, with or without irony. The use of such foreign terms, often implying not only geographical but also chronological distance, can suggest a desire to disown something as 'really' part of one's society, as Judith Hallett has argued in the case of ancient Rome.[11] But is her observation valid *only* for ancient Rome? Historicizing claims about the past tend to occlude their potential predication of the present – their inevitable predication of the present, if the past is constructed in terms of present concerns – and the use of foreign terms emerges as one manifestation of a powerful

[9] MacMullen (1982), 485.   [10] MacMullen (1982), 488; italics mine.
[11] Hallett (1989).

ideological myth that whatever is viewed with anxiety has been brought in from outside; think of the way the French refer to male sexual relations with male as 'the English vice' or the English refer to condoms as 'French letters', or, more sinisterly, the ideological charge involved in associating the earliest AIDS cases with Africa.[12] MacMullen accepts this ideological myth as representing the truth by the use of phrases like 'importation' and 'as much at home', and he accommodates his analysis to two essentialisms, namely that there is a thing called homosexuality, and that it is in some way essentially Greek. He ends his article by observing that same-sex activities were largely confined to the upper classes (he singles out Catullus and Tibullus for comment): 'The resistance [homosexuality] met tells us that all other parts of the citizen body, notably the non-rich and those who weren't elbow-to-elbow with Greek neighbours, were little affected.'[13] The problem with this approach is not only that these two essentialisms are taken for granted as self-evidently true; as we have seen, what the discourse of sexuality renders problematic is this very essentializing process of thought as a whole. It is, of course, still *possible* in the light of the current discourse of sexuality to ask the question 'was Tibullus a homosexual?', but it is now open to us to wonder how worthwhile it is, for given the projection of such terms as of descriptive, transhistorical validity, it will always be possible to discover in the historical archive of antiquity 'evidence' of behaviour or psychology amenable to classification in these terms.[14]

But before we investigate further the problematics of essentializing, let us pause to consider what a reading of elegy accommodated to the concerns of these contemporary discourses of sexuality and gender would look like. One recent intervention emphasizes that its formulations do not purport to describe what the experience of sex was 'really' like for members of ancient societies, but to indicate how it is *represented* in the utterances and actions of free adult males which constitute the historical archive,[15] and thus to render visible once more the distinctions effaced by modern categories. Sex, as portrayed from this perspective and

---

[12] The positive connotations of 'foreignness' are also, of course, available for appropriation, as when Oscar Wilde exploited the associations of 'Greek' in Victorian England to refer to male homoerotic desire as 'Greek love'.

[13] MacMullen (1982), 501; the rhetoric suggests that what he is talking about might be contagious.   [14] See Halperin (1990), 28.

[15] See Halperin (1990), 30; the terms of his formulation are, of course, open to the kind of analysis discussed in ch. 1 above.

in these terms in this archive, is an action performed by one person upon another, radically asymmetrical in that it is conceived to consist essentially in the penetration of the body of one person by the body of another, and thus polarizing its participants as 'active' (i.e. insertive) and 'passive' (receptive).[16] The categories of active and passive used to describe sexual behaviour become organized along lines of gender, active being 'essentially' male and passive 'essentially' female, in such a way that it becomes meaningful for a Roman author to speak of a man who submits to the passive role in intercourse with another man by the phrase *muliebria pati* (Sallust, *Catiline* 13.3), to undergo the woman's role. Within this scheme, the situation so frequently depicted in Roman elegy, a man subdued and enslaved by love for a woman presented as playing the dominant role in the relationship, enacts an inversion of these conventional gender stereotypes. This could be illustrated more specifically by looking once more at Propertius 1.7.

The Latin adjectives *durus*, 'hard', and *mollis*, 'soft', were so gender-specific, male and female respectively, that the noun *mollitia*, 'softness', could be used without more ado to describe derogatively male behaviour that was thought to contain characteristics essentially female. Thus the historian Velleius Paterculus describes the notorious lifestyle of the literary patron Maecenas as follows:

> ubi res vigiliam exigeret, sane insomnis, providens atque agendi sciens; simul vero aliquid ex negotio remitti posset, otio ac mollitiis paene ultra feminam fluens. (2.88.2)

> when circumstances demanded alertness, he would do without sleep completely, show foresight and know what needed to be done; but the moment there was any opportunity of relaxing from pressure, he would dissolve into an idleness and acts of softness almost beyond what one would expect of a woman.

Within an androcentric discourse, as soon as you say 'she' you say sex, because 'you' are male and for you 'she' means 'sex',[17] so *mollitia* and related terms inevitably entail erotic connotations as well; conversely *durus* bears a male erotic sense. Propertius 1.7 offers an elaborate play on these adjectives which involves an inversion of their conventional gender associations. In line 6, the female *domina*, mistress, is described as *dura*,

---

[16] See Veyne (1985); Halperin (1990), 30.
[17] See Henderson (1989); I owe the formulation in this sentence to Alison Sharrock.

hard, which invokes the elegiac situation of the woman as dominant. This is only the starting-point, however, for the gendered opposition of *mollis* and *durus* ramifies into literary reference as well. The addressee of the poem, Ponticus, is presented to us as an epic poet writing the story of Thebes, a poem in the Homeric epic tradition (1–4). This sets the scene for Propertius' definition of elegy: if Cupid strikes you with his bow, he tells Ponticus (15), in vain you'll wish to compose *soft* verse (*mollem componere versum*, 19), and Amor, called in too late, will not supply you with poems (*nec tibi subiciet carmina serus Amor*, 20). So, elegy is defined by means of *mollis*, which discursively aligns itself with the feminine, whilst epic is by implication aligned with the masculine, and elsewhere is characterized as *durus*.[18] Given the dramatic situation it enacts and the lover's role within it in relation to his mistress, the verse he writes must be *mollis*.[19] The verb applied to Cupid, *subicere*, is elsewhere used of positioning in the passive role for sexual intercourse,[20] so the act of poetic composition about erotic themes is itself figured in terms of a sexual act, and writing is subsumed into erotic experience. Thus, in wishing for the success of Ponticus' epic, Propertius hopes that the fates will prove to be *mollia*, compliant, to his (masculine) poem (4). The lover, on the other hand, as is his wont . . . does what? *nos, ut consuemus, nostros agitamus amores|atque aliquid duram quaerimus in dominam* (5f.): is he occupied with his love-affair,[21] trying to find something to 'soften' his 'hard'-hearted mistress, or with writing poetry, searching out ways of representing a 'hard' mistress in 'soft' verse? He is obliged, he says, to be a slave not so much to his talent as to his pain (7f.), and to bewail the 'hard' times of his youth (*aetatis tempora dura queri*). As a *man* whose *domina*, whether that signifies 'woman of flesh-and-blood' or 'woman as subject-matter', is not compliant, his times are 'hard' in respect of unresolved desire, and the verb 'to bewail' (*queri*) becomes discursively constructed to signify the act of writing elegy. The terms of literary description and analysis, even the structure of that analysis, emerge from this approach

---

[18] Cf. e.g. Prop. 2.1.41, 3.1.19–20.

[19] On the figuring of the technical rhetorical term *compositio* as sexual activity in Roman literature in general, and in Hor. *Sat.* 2.1 in particular, see Freudenberg (1990), 197–203. *compositio* deemed over-elaborate was seen as a sign of 'effeminacy', most notably in the case of Maecenas, Sen. *Ep.* 114.8.

[20] Cf. Suet. *Jul.* 7.2.

[21] On the applicability of the verb *agitare* to both communal and solitary sexual activity see Adams (1982), 144–5.

as incorporating assumptions about the nature of sexual identity. This approach is, of course, no less applicable to contemporary terminology than to Roman; to what extent was my argument in chapter 1 underpinned by the use of a biological male and a biological female respectively as representatives of what were termed 'hard' and 'soft' historicism? The conventional attributes of 'masculinity' and 'femininity' shape our sense of arguments and writing, but only become 'visible' when literary analysis reflexively questions its sexual rhetoric, a theme that will be pursued further in the next chapter. From the viewpoint of gender studies, the means of representing literature become objects of representation in their own right. If treated as 'purely' analytical terms rather than as objects of analysis, the conventional gender associations they encode remain unexamined.

If the gendered opposition of *mollis* and *durus* ramifies into literary definition, it also ramifies into social distinction, a cardinal issue in the current discourse of sexuality. Foucault asserts that 'sexual relations – always conceived in terms of the model act of penetration, assuming a polarity that opposed activity and passivity – were seen as being of the same type as the relationship between a superior and a subordinate, an individual who dominates and one who is dominated, one who commands and one who complies, one who vanquishes and one who is vanquished';[22] and Halperin, discussing classical Athens, observes that an adult male citizen could have legitimate sexual relations only with inferiors in social and political status (women, boys, foreigners, slaves), and that 'what a citizen does in bed reflects the differential in status that distinguishes him from his sexual partner: the citizen's superior prestige and authority express themselves in his sexual precedence – in his power to initiate a sexual act, his right to obtain pleasure from it, and his assumption of an insertive rather than a receptive sexual role.'[23] A constant theme of Paul Veyne's work on the Romans is the connection between 'virility' and social dignity.[24] In the first poem of Propertius 1, subjection to a mistress who is *dura* by implication of her comparison to the mythical Atalanta (*durae . . . Iasidos*, 10) is depicted in terms of loss of social status: the lover describes himself as deserving the treatment normally meted out to slaves (27–8). By the behaviour depicted, subjection to a woman, he represents himself as though he has forfeited

---

[22] Foucault (1986b), 215.   [23] Halperin (1990), 30–1.
[24] Veyne (1978); (1985); (1987).

his right to the social distinctions that were only open to free men, and has become degraded to the only status lower than that of a woman, the status of slave.

However, the conclusions to be drawn from a text such as this for the 'realities' of Roman society or of the life of a member of its élite in love are not self-evident. What are perceived as the realities of Roman social and political life have proved to be rather fluid, as fluid as the definition of 'political'. Consideration of the use of this term will give further purchase on the issue of essentialism. Writing of Catullus and the elegists in 1968, Gordon Williams posed the question: 'How did they treat the real world in their poetry? For this purpose the real world will be limited to that of state and politics and the Empire.'[25] This quotation is revealing both in what it deems 'politics' to be and also for the way that political ideologies have shifted since it was written. 'Politics' is projected as referring only to formal institutions (the state, the Empire) and the personalities directly involved in them. Williams continues: 'This is the world in which Propertius sets his love-poetry: it is created out of a tension between the real world of politics and the private microcosm of his love-affair.'[26] The phrases 'the real world of politics' and 'the private microcosm of his love-affair' set up a contrast between 'real' and 'private' which is produced within a discourse in which 'sexuality' and 'politics' are deemed to be autonomous categories, separate spheres of activity which will normally not impinge upon each other, and they exemplify an ideology of sexuality as 'private' which was widespread at the time that Williams was writing, being enshrined, for example in the act passed in Britain in 1967 legalizing sexual acts between consenting adult males 'in private'. Even within the limits of this definition of the 'political', divergent interpretations can be developed, and 'facts' established which are deemed to underpin those interpretations. Thus Williams, discussing Propertius 2.1, says that the poet 'shares with Horace and Virgil the characteristically Augustan adaptation of the *recusatio*',[27] reading the poem as an expression of adherence to Maecenas and Augustus rather than as a statement of unwillingness to conform. On the basis of this, Propertius is described as 'clearly a member of the group of poets in the circle of Maecenas'.[28] The assumption is that Propertius is a love poet, a personal poet, and so it is inconceivable that this could represent serious

---

[25] Williams (1968), 557.   [26] Williams (1968), 558.

[27] Williams (1968), 557–8.   [28] Williams (1968), 558.

political dissent; and poetry isn't, of course, political, except when it deals with matters of state. These assumptions allow Williams to describe it as a 'novel touch' that Propertius 'ends one book with a searching re-creation of the miseries of Perusia [1.22] and begins the next [2.1] with a grand address to Maecenas, in which he expounds the epic quality of the events of Roman history, but particularly those since the murder of Caesar (he includes Perusia in the list, 2.1.29)'.[29] Similarly, in dealing with 2.16, he sees no discrepancy between what he describes as the 'conventional' account of Actium there and his statement in the very next sentence that 'elsewhere in his love-poetry Propertius condemns Actium as such'.[30] The ideologies which underpin the approach of Williams produce a reading of Propertius in which there are no discrepancies or contradictions, or at least none that are deemed to matter. Their appearance in love-poetry presumably renders condemnations of Actium neutral, whilst the invocation of terms such as 'conventional', with its reassuring etymological associations of 'coming together' and 'agreement', has a flattening effect, implying that regardless of the context in which an utterance is made, its significance will always be the same for those concerned.[31] Similarly, the ostensibly 'objective', formal term *recusatio*, through what is described as a 'characteristically Augustan adaptation',[32] serves to obliterate any notions of dissent or conflict, the very notions that in the ideological framework within which Williams is operating would require the application of the term 'political'.[33]

Just as the text of Propertius can be processed by its readers in such a way as to minimalize and iron out any 'discrepancies' or 'contradictions', which might be construed in terms of 'opposition' or 'dissent', so it can be processed in such a way as to generate and emphasize them. For example, Hans-Peter Stahl reads the poems of Propertius as the expression of an individual's beliefs and sensibility, in order to get to know Propertius as a personality, an individual. Within a biographical framework, what are perceived as discrepancies or inconsistencies can be explained as, for example, a change of mind, but, as Stahl himself points out, the terms in which this is put are never less than loaded. Thus he draws attention to the way in which the career of Propertius, the poet who writes of the sack of Perusia in 1.22 and celebrates the Battle of Actium in 4.6, has been characterized as a 'development' to a 'mature' Augustan stance.[34] The

---

[29] Williams (1968), 558.   [30] Williams (1968), 559.   [31] See Kennedy, (1992), 36–7.
[32] Williams (168), 558.   [33] See Kennedy (1992), 30.   [34] Stahl (1985), 368.

assumption behind such rhetoric is that no sane person could have thought that Augustus was ever anything other than inevitable and necessary and a good thing for Rome, and that the rebellious young Propertius eventually saw sense and did his duty. Stahl characterizes this way of reading Propertius as adopting the perspectives of what he terms 'Augustan Interpretation': the reader internalizes Augustan ideology and reads the poetry from that viewpoint. Stahl offers a different perspective: Propertius remained hostile to Augustus throughout his life, but he became subject to increasing pressure to conform, to become a mouthpiece for the Augustan world-view. Thus, according to this line of interpretation, the *recusatio* addressed to Maecenas in 2.1 signifies not a coded expression of willingness to conform, but a protest against the demand to conform. Poems which present an apparently Augustan perspective, for example on the subject of the Battle of Actium, testify, Stahl argues, to the intensity of the pressure being brought to bear on the poet; periodically the pose he is being forced to adopt breaks down and the 'real' Propertius, the anti-Augustan Propertius, speaks out once more, either within whole poems or in details which are interpreted as incongruous in a poem otherwise characterized as pro-Augustan.

There are difficulties with this approach, however. First, Stahl constructs from the text of Propertius an extra-textual individual whom he essentializes as 'anti-Augustan', and then reads the poems as that individual's response to external pressures. A prevailing assumption or ideology of many contemporary Western societies (all the more powerful for being identified with, and taken for granted as being, the truth, and thus pervading political thinking and the structures which that helps to generate) is that people are individuals who are essentially this or essentially that, and that this essence pre-exists events and reacts with them. This ideology of the individual pervades Stahl's book and finds its way into the sub-title, 'Individual *and* State'. However, this is *a* theory, *an* ideology, of personality which is not uncontested, and is always open to the argument that personality is not an essence which pre-exists experience, but is actively being constructed and re-constructed within the discourses in which people participate. Second, Stahl presents the Augustan perspective, Augustan Interpretation, as monolithic, suggesting that there were and are certain views, certain standpoints essentially Augustan. But all definitions of 'ideology' are constructed from a standpoint (are thus themselves 'ideological'), and although 'ideology' is frequently reified in this way, it cannot wholly occlude the possibility of representing 'ideology' as not monolithic but generated out of a process of constant contestation. Within this relativizing approach, 'Augustus' is viewed not as an individual but as a figure who was (and continues to be) a focus, an embodiment, of conflicting and often contradictory discourses,[35] and everybody, not least Augustus, had to negotiate a position within them, a process involving all kinds of anxieties and uncertainties, as for example when the figure who was the focus for a discourse of moral regeneration at Rome found himself with an adulteress for a daughter. From this perspective, power is never an absolute, but is always generated out of what it depicts itself as needing to control, and figures of power must constantly negotiate their position within the discourses which constitute them as a focus of power. What Propertius wrote has always been open to appropriation to serve different interests. If poem 2.15 were read as, say, suggesting that the Battle of Actium should never have happened (cf. 41–6), this reading itself is open to appropriation in a way that could have served Augustus, for example by characterizing the poem as the ravings of a debauched rake, the very sort of attitudes Augustus was propelled into power to control.

Thus what is deemed to fall within the rubric 'politics in ancient poetry' is not simply determined by the ancient texts (as the rubric seems to imply) but is organized in accordance with what is and is not deemed 'political' within the ideological perspective of the interpreter. 'Politics' (and no less its converse 'not-politics') is easily reified; the assertion that a belief, practice or institution is *essentially* 'political' (or 'not-political') obscures the degree to which 'disagreements about the scope and domain of "the political" are themselves constitutive features of political discourse'.[36] Although it frequently aligns itself with the 'not-political', scholarship can always be represented as a participant in this discourse and as itself one vehicle for the reproduction, legitimation or criticism of ideologies that constitute and shape the society within which it operates. Thus the ideology of sexuality as 'private' which informs Williams' treatment in 1968 appropriates, reifies and projects, as a relatively unproblematic opposition to the 'public' sphere ('politics'), the Catullan

---

[35] See Kennedy (1992), 35, 40–1.

[36] Ball (1988), 13. The statement might well be expanded to include 'agreements' as well as 'disagreements'. As it stands, it reflects an ideological assumption that the 'proper' sphere of reference of the term 'politics' is issues of conflict, difference and disruption. Agreement and integration are no less 'political' in the sense that they affect the distribution of power in specific contexts.

and elegiac discourse of amatory *otium*. This discourse was no less available for appropriation in the early 1970s to project the *otium* of elegy admiringly as 'counter-cultural'.[37] Throughout that decade, feminism was playing a leading role in deconstructing conventional distinctions between 'public' and 'private' with a view to revealing the part such distinctions play in the cultural construction of gender roles, and the interests served thereby.[38] From being opposed to the 'political', the 'private' now *became* the 'political', allowing what used to be the problematic of 'sex *and* politics' to be transmuted into 'sexual politics'. For Stahl, encoding elegy in terms of the ideological anxieties of late twentieth-century (male) liberalism, the intrusion of the 'public' into the 'private' is a central theme, but the distinction is recuperated in terms of a reading of the poetry of Propertius as opposing two lifestyles signified by 'love' and 'war', with 'love' coming to represent 'the last . . . bastion of the individual for defending himself against the homogenizing forces of an authoritarian rule'.[39] Meanwhile, for Maria Wyke, cautioning against the appropriation of elegy to underpin suggestions of the emergence of a type of 'emancipated' behaviour on the part of some women in Rome at the time, 'the heterodoxy of the elegiac portrayal of love . . . lies in the absence of a political or social role for the male narrator, not in any attempt to provide or demand a political role for the female subject . . . The elegiac poets exploit the traditional methods of ordering female sexuality which locate the sexually unrestrained and therefore socially ineffective female on the margins of society in order to portray their first-person heroes as displaced from a central position in the social categories of Augustan Rome. And moreover', she concludes, 'they evaluate that displacement in conventional terms . . . the poetic depiction of subjection to a mistress is aligned, in a conventional moral framework, with depravity.'[40] Within her scheme, the discourse of *otium* has become thoroughly 'politicized' – not as 'oppositional' or 'counter-cultural', but as a signifier of the reproduction of hegemonic gender roles.

When issues of sexuality and gender are inscribed within a discourse of 'politics', a range of representations from the 'oppositional' to the 'integrative' are available within which critics are able to map their appropriations and position themselves. The case of Maecenas can once again illustrate the breadth of potential interpretation. Roman texts

---

[37] See Hallett (1973); Sullivan (1976). [38] Greene and Kahn (1985), 15–17.
[39] Stahl (1985), 147. [40] Wyke (1989a), 42–3.

regularly present his lifestyle as the epitome of *mollitia* in dress and in behaviour, exemplified by a passionate love-affair with a male actor named Bathyllus.[41] Accusations of *mollitia* need not have done him social harm even in a society in which masculinity was apparently so aligned with superiority as in the Roman, and he can be represented as having appropriated the discourse of *mollitia* to his own benefit. Within such a discursive situation, the adoption by a male social élite, or a member of it, of a style perceived in gender terms as pejoratively effeminate can be seen as a very effective means of reinforcing a distinction between the élite and other social classes, or within the élite itself, as Pierre Bourdieu has argued,[42] using the example of accent in his native France: the accents and articulatory style of upper-class males are often described or mimicked by members of other social classes in terms which pejoratively suggest effeminacy. The assumption of masculinity as the norm leads to a rejection of their own accord by those other classes of the stylistic strategies of the upper classes, thus reinforcing the class distinction even, arguably, against their own interests.

What thus emerges as constantly at issue in the discourses of sexuality and gender is the essentializing process of thought as a whole: *is* there a 'thing' that transcends history called 'sexuality' or 'gender'? The feminist movement was instrumental in bringing into question not only the assumption that certain qualities are essentially masculine or feminine but the means by which this way of thinking operates. Feminists differ as to what they wish to do with these arguments. Some, having destabilized the male/female hierarchy of values, would wish to maintain that some qualities remain essentially masculine or feminine, except that now the values attached to them have been re-assessed; others would wish to continue the critique of essentialism; and so the discourse continues and ramifies. The significance of essentializing arguments remains open to appropriation in different ways by divergent interests, and starts also to articulate differences *within* feminism as well as between feminism and other discourses. Nor is it any longer unproblematic to make the glib assumption that essentializing thought is somehow reactionary and critiques of it progressive; the idea that one mode of thought must be progressive and another reactionary is itself an act of essentializing. John Boswell's 'liberal' thesis, encoded in the title of his book *Christianity,*

---

[41] Cf. Tac. *Ann.* 1.54.3; an innuendo along this line was also alleged by the ancient scholiast on Horace's Fourteenth *Epode*, which is addressed to Maecenas and has as its opening word *mollis*.   [42] Bourdieu (1982), 90.

Social Tolerance and Homosexuality: Gay People in Western Europe from the Beginning of the Christian Era to the Fourteenth Century,[43] is founded on an essentialism, social tolerance, that he projects back into the ancient world. Some gay activists view the abandonment of an 'essentializing' view of homosexuality with anxiety. For them it is important that they are gay 'by nature' rather than through 'cultural influence', and they are apprehensive that an intellectually 'progressive' position which says that sexual preference is culturally rather than naturally determined leaves them vulnerable to those who would 're-educate' them to be heterosexual and censor anything regarded as promoting homosexuality.[44] Foucault's pessimism serves to warn that an intervention that presents itself in the rhetoric of emancipation or liberation is an intervention in the discourse, not the imminent arrival of Freedom with a capital F, but part of a continuing struggle over meaning, knowledge and power. Whilst we may be brought to abandon certain categories, others will take their place, whilst others again will have altered their definitions, and their discursive function, often beyond our immediate notice.

In presenting 'homosexuality' as a cultural construct of comparatively recent provenance, Halperin acknowledges that he is positioning himself controversially within the discourse. In answer to John Boswell's observation that 'if the categories "homosexual/heterosexual", "gay/straight" are the inventions of particular societies rather than real aspects of the human psyche, there is no gay history',[45] he argues that, rather than attempting to trace the history of 'homosexuality' as if it were a *thing*, projecting it as a descriptive category of transhistorical validity, 'the *real* issue confronting the cultural historian of antiquity, and any critic of contemporary culture, is, first of all, how to recover the terms in which the experiences of individuals belonging to past societies were *actually* constituted, and second, how to measure and assess the differences between these terms and the ones we currently employ.' The result, he says, will not be gay history in the sense of the history of people viewed as essentially gay, but rather history written from the perspective of contemporary gay interests, just as feminist history is not the history of women but history that reflects the concerns of contemporary feminism.[46] However, there is a bind in this critique of essentializing terms of

[43] Boswell (1980).   [44] See Halperin (1990), 51–3.

[45] Boswell (1982/3), 93, cited by Halperin (1990), 18, who notes that Boswell himself rejects the view.   [46] See Halperin (1990), 29; italics mine.

which Halperin is not unaware. In order to project sexuality or gender as culturally constructed and historically specific, it is necessary to project 'sexuality' and 'gender' as analytical terms of universal and transhistorical validity. Representing the past as fundamentally 'different' involves projecting it at some level, however occluded, as also fundamentally the 'same'. As Halperin admits, in the course of implementing the ostensibly radical project of writing the history of sexuality as an interrogation of the very naturalness of what we currently take to be essential to our individual natures, 'many historians of sexuality seem to have reversed – perhaps unwittingly – its radical design: by preserving "sexuality" as a stable category of historical analysis, not only have they not denaturalized it but on the contrary they have newly idealized it ... To the extent that ... histories of "sexuality" succeed in concentrating their focus on *sexuality*, to just that extent are they doomed to failure as *histories*' in that they occlude the historicity of their own categories of analysis.[47] This is a bind from which we cannot escape, however. Any term, any definition has both an essentializing and a relativizing dimension. For example, Ball's relativizing definition cited above ('Disagreements about the scope and domain of "the political" are themselves constitutive features of political discourse') presents 'the political' as an *essentially* contested term; conversely, essentializing definitions are always open to representation in terms of their occluded specificity, as I have done in the case of Williams' definition of 'the political'. All relativizing discourses and definitions will invoke, at some level and however provisionally, essentializing notions, and *vice versa*, whatever ostensible positions are adopted. This renders problematical any ultimate appeal to essentialism, for example in gender studies, whether it be the long-established search amongst classical scholars for traces of 'Feminine Latinity' in the Sulpicia poems[48] or Hélène Cixous's 'écriture feminine' or Luce Irigaray's 'womanspeak'.[49] The assertion of univocal male or female discourses or readings,[50] or references to discourse as 'androcentric', have a strategic function in context but no claims to transcendental truth. 'Woman' and 'man' do not have an unproblematic referential status as essentials, but are figures of speech, always signs of something else. For example, in gender studies, '"woman" has come to

---

[47] Halperin (1990), 40; the italics are Halperin's.
[48] See Smith (1913), 80–1.   [49] See Moi (1985), 113–26; 144–5.
[50] See e.g. Gamel (1989) on Ovid's abortion poems (*Am.* 2.13 and 14).

stand for any radical force that subverts the concepts, assumptions and structures of traditional male discourse'.[51] As figures of speech, they are always involved in rhetorical manipulation. Halperin's anti-essentializing investigation of Plato's enunciation in the voice of a woman of a doctrine of male homoerotic desire in the *Symposium* (inevitably) concludes with a rejection of those questions which demand essentializing answers: 'And so to ask why Diotima is a woman is to pose a question that ultimately has no answer.'[52] The body too is never simply a thing-in-itself, but always functions also as a trope. This is frequently elided, however, as in Foucault's search for a pre-modern 'experience of the flesh' as against the modern 'experience of sexuality', which seeks to ground itself in a rhetorical appeal to the bare essentials.

Halperin is remarkably sensitive to this bind, though of course he cannot evade it, but he does succeed in pushing the problem one stage back (a process of deferral which is arguably all anybody can hope to achieve), using strategies that are familiar from chapter 1 above. Instead of concentrating on the history of sexuality, he suggests, 'we need to define and refine a new, and radical, historical sociology of psychology',[53] i.e. a fresh discourse of the 'real', projected by the techniques of realism which, under the pressure of textualist challenge, have migrated (and been transformed in the process) from conventional history to sociology. The new rhetoric of the 'real', whilst deeming our own cultural assumptions *'inappropriate'* to the interpretation of sexual life in ancient Greece, nonetheless holds out the possibility of recovering some of the *'indigenous* meanings attached to sexual experiences in ancient Greece if only we do not insist on viewing the ancient documents through the prism of modern social and sexual categories'.[54] But the ancient world is represented from within the contestation of 'our own cultural assumptions', and thus the term 'inappropriate' serves to articulate and determine a particular approach in pursuit of a certain end as legitimate.[55] Halperin goes on to suggest that 'we must acknowledge that "sexuality" is a cultural production no less than table manners ... and we must struggle to discern in what we currently regard as our most precious, unique, original and most spontaneous impulses the traces of a previously *rehearsed* and socially encoded ideological *script*.'[56] Individ-

---

[51] Culler (1983), 61.   [52] Halperin (1990), 151.   [53] Halperin (1990), 40.
[54] Halperin (1990), 10; italics mine.
[55] On notions of 'propriety' see further ch. 3 below.
[56] Halperin (1990), 40; italics mine.

uals are represented as em*body*ing in their actions specific discourses of sexuality, thus allowing Halperin to argue of classical Athens that 'sex was a manifestation of personal status, a declaration of social identity; sexual behaviour did not so much express inward dispositions or inclinations . . . as it served to position social *actors* in the places assigned to them, by virtue of their political standing, in the Athenian polity . . . sex between social superior and social inferior was a miniature *drama* of polarization which served to measure and define the social distance between them.'[57] From the perspective of gay studies, in which the conventional conceptual division between 'sexuality' and 'politics' has been challenged, sexual behaviour and gender identity, far from being 'private', *enact* politics. This discourse of sexuality shifts the major constituent of identity from an inherent 'sexuality' to social positionality. 'Politics', thus freshly defined to incorporate notions of gender and sexual behaviour, is reified as the new horizon of interpretation, and texts are read and appropriated accordingly. A favourite text of the current discourse of sexuality is the work on the interpretation of dreams by Artemidorus in which dreams about sex are interpreted as being 'really' about social prestige and political status: the tenor of signification is *from* sex *to* politics, reversing that familiar from Freud.[58]

'Love' is no less (though perhaps less obviously) the focus for contestation; its status as an 'essential' has been less subject to examination, but it could no less than the categories of sexuality and gender be represented as historically specific in its manifestations, with each age trying to impose its definition, only to find the word, like Ovid's winged Amor, taking to flight again. The Romantic Age made a notable attempt to define love, so much so that the assumptions underlying its usage even now, those of sincerity, sensitivity and the notion that one's personality finds its ultimate identity in passionate affective emotion, remain predominantly 'Romantic'. This is at any rate the notion that underlies so many contemporary approaches to Roman elegy and provides the criteria for judging it. Such a view marginalizes the 'passionless' and 'dreamy' Tibullus and elevates Propertius over Ovid, who, read in Romantic terms, is described as 'heartless' or, the ultimate crime again Romantic sincerity, 'frivolous'. The Romantic definition of 'love' has been under explicit attack, and not just discursive contestation,

---

[57] Halperin (1990), 32; italics mine.
[58] See Halperin (1990), 37; Price (1990); Winkler (1990), 17–44; and ch. 3 below on tenors of signification.

43

for at least a century now, and yet it still maintains a tenacious hold on our responses, thanks in part to the unproblematic romanticism that has been appropriated by commercial interests, like advertizing and popular music, to saturate our lives. In a world experienced as dominated by pressure and uncertainty, the myth of Romantic love offers an alluring fantasy of escape, even to those who regard it as a myth. It has been fashionable (i.e. a useful positional ploy) for some time now to express exasperation at the triteness of the notion of Romantic love and proclaim us all 'post-Romantics' now. Such a view finds its validation in the way that it can now appreciate the sexual frankness and humour of Ovid's 'explicit' siesta poem, *Amores* 1.5, and can laugh at the studied exercise in insincerity that *Amores* 1.3 is now read as. But are these expressions of exasperation and worldly-wisdom the mark of a culture that has left Romantic notions behind? Or are they evidence of the power of Romantic discourse to perpetuate its categories of evaluation, albeit by inversion? But to be drawn into the debate in this way, like all debates over the status of, or our position in relation to, any 'post -isms', is to revert to an unproblematic essentialism.

In adding to the essentializing question '*what* does *amor*/"love" mean?' the supplement '*how* does *amor*/"love" mean?', I offered the concept of a discourse of Roman love elegy, in which the 'text' of elegy stands for, *means*, all the forces that moulded the text plus the appropriations that constitute its reception. We are only able to read elegy from within this discourse, and within it, as Charles Martindale has suggested to me, the distinction between 'reading' and 'reading into' is deconstructed. In rendering Propertius 1.7.19, *et frustra cupies mollem componere versum*, a recent translator offers: 'In vain you'll wish to write *romantic* verse.'[59] For this to emerge as a viable, meaningful rendering, there has had to be a monumental act of cultural processing, involving thousands of people over many generations as well as processes of appropriation we ignore at our peril. Just as Ovid's Amor is able to wander all over the world, we might rephrase our questions to read: 'What *cannot amor*/"love" mean?' and 'What discursive areas *cannot amor*/"love" be a signifier of?' We might even ask, as Ovid indignantly enquires of Cupid in *Amores* 1.1.15, *an, quod ubique, tuum est*? ('is it true that everything everywhere is yours?'), so long as we are prepared for the reply that anything whatsoever can be articulated in and through the language of *amor*/

---

[59] Shepherd (1985), 42; italics mine.

'love'. The search for the essential meaning of love, so long deferred within this chapter, has led to the (provisional) conclusion that it is essentially contested, essentially mobile. A number of the issues raised here will be resumed, temporarily at least, in the context of a lover's discourse in chapter 4 below. Meanwhile, the rhetorical construction of this radical, conceptually destablizing alterity should soften or harden the reader up so that s/he is ready to proceed to the next chapter.

3

Love's figures and tropes

When we set out to describe some thing or experience, we inevitably find ourselves using terms that are also applicable to other things or experiences. Think of the way we talk about arguments and theories. Arguments may be *without foundation*; it may be necessary to *build up* more evidence to *support* a theory, or *shore up* an argument to prevent it being *undermined*, or *collapsing* or being *demolished*. In English, one way of describing an argument is in terms which can also be used to describe buildings. Arguments are *constructed*, and, these days, *deconstructed*; they may be said to have, or lack, *structure*. There are other ways: it is possible to talk of arguments in terms also used to describe war. In an argument, an *opponent* can *attack* an idea; an argument can be *challenged, defended, won* and *lost*; an argument can be said to be *tactical* or a *strategy*. This can be taken one step further. If an argument is described as *labyrinthine*, its complexity is suggested by the use of an adjective that recalls the most anfractuous of buildings, out of which Theseus had to find his way; the use of the word to describe an argument also alludes to the way that the process of argumentation is described in terms also applicable to traversing ground. I have articulated this argument by saying 'there are other *ways*' and 'this can be taken *one step further*'. One can talk of *making headway* or *progress* or *getting bogged down* in an argument. And, combining the last two notions, in describing arguments one can use words that are also used to describe warfare in spatial terms: in arguments, one can be said to *gain ground* or *retreat from one's position*; it may even be necessary to resort to a *last-ditch* argument.[1]

---

[1] See Lakoff and Johnson (1980), from whom a number of these and the following examples are taken.

Talking about love similarly involves using terms that are also applicable to other things. For instance, love can be described in terms also used for madness: 'I'm *crazy* about you'; 'he's always *raving* about her'; 'they're *mad* about each other'. Or illness: 'he's *getting over* her now'; 'their relationship is *on its last legs*'. Or magic: 'she *cast her spell over* him'; 'she is *charming, entrancing*'; 'I'm *bewitched* by her smile'; 'that *old black magic* called love'. Popular songs can be a very good source for usages like this, for in their lyrics they often alight upon a common way of speaking about love and develop humourous or piquant variations on it. Or a physical force, like gravity: 'when I *fall* in love'; 'her life *revolves around* him'; or magnetism: 'fatal *attraction*'; or electricity: 'they *sparked* it off immediately'; 'theirs is a *highly-charged* relationship'. Or a journey: 'we've *come a long way* together'; 'they have decided to *go* their separate *ways*'; 'they felt their relationship wasn't *getting anywhere*'; 'their marriage is *on the rocks*'; 'their affair *came off the rails*'; 'let's *go the whole way*'; and, for a climax, the late twentieth century's favourite term, 'to *come*'. Or war: 'she *fled* from his *advances*'; 'he has made another *conquest*'; 'with a sigh, she *surrendered* to his embrace'.

Love can be described in terms that are also applicable to a journey or to war; so, as we saw above, can an argument. The range of applicability of some words is thus very wide, in Latin no less than in English. Let us consider briefly the first poem of Propertius' first book in the light of this. Cynthia, it begins, first *captured* with her eyes my pitiable self (*Cynthia prima suis miserum me cepit ocellis*). The verb *cepit* can also be found in military and hunting contexts, so it could be said that love is being described in terms also applicable to war or hunting, and interpretative strategies can be developed from this observation. Thus, from a gender perspective, it could be argued that the uses of the verb *capere* in such contexts lead to an expectation that the subject of the verb is going to be male, but with Cynthia as its subject the elegiac inversion of gender stereotypes, the domination of the lover by his mistress, is already adumbrated. Alternatively one could argue that *capere* is also a term which can describe magical entrapment, and so relate it to a discourse in which power is unusually gendered as female. Interpretation will be determined/enabled by the applicability of the verb and the ideological perspective of the interpreter. The lover continues by describing his 'pitiable self' as 'touched before by no desires' (2). The verb *contingere* is used also of catching a disease, and so love for Cynthia can be said to be spoken of in the same terms as an illness, and one could point out, as a development of this, the use in line 7 of the word *furor* to refer to his love, 'this *madness* has not left me for a whole year now'. In English, mood is often conveyed through terms of direction or orientation, with happiness being signified by 'up' (as in 'things are *looking up*', 'on a *high*'), and sadness by 'down' (as in '*down* in the dumps'); often the use of Latinisms (as in 'elated' or 'depressed') serves to obscure or defer one stage awareness of the sense of orientation involved. Propertius 1.1.3–4,

> tum mihi constantis deiecit lumina fastus
> et caput impositis pressit Amor pedibus

> then Love cast down my look of constant disdain, placed his foot on my head and pressed down

graphically creates a miniature drama of the humiliation (cf. *humus*, 'ground') and subjection (cf. *subicere*, 'throw down') that love for Cynthia has brought with it. Amor has cast down the lover's erstwhile *haughty* glance and stands triumphant over him with his foot pressing the lover's neck to the ground, a gesture that is often associated in Roman texts with victory in single combat. In 9ff., the lover compares his situation with that of the mythical Milanion, who was prepared to undergo any hardship, including the perils of hunting monsters, and by so doing was able to tame (*domuisse*, 15) Atalanta, sexual domination being expressed by a term also used in the sphere of hunting. However, Love does not remember to follow his familiar route as he used to (17f.); a relationship can be viewed in the same terms as a journey in Latin no less than in English. Witchcraft proving of no help to him, the lover appeals to his friends to seek out help for his sick or crazed heart (*non sani pectoris*, 26); the term *sanus* could equally suggest physical or mental illness. Surgery and cauterization were standard remedies for illness or madness, and the lover states that he will bravely suffer knife and fire, if only he has the freedom to speak what his anger wishes:

> fortiter et ferrum saevos patiemur et ignis,
> sit modo libertas quae velit ira loqui   (27–8)

A sphere other than illness is also simultaneously suggested by these terms. The testimony of slaves was admitted in Roman courts only if it had been extracted under torture. The terms used present the lover both as insane and as enslaved by love to Cynthia. Interpreters may for whatever reason highlight one rather than the other, but both are available.

Love, as we have seen, can be described in terms which are also applicable to journeys; thus in Propertius 3.24.15–16 the lover looks back upon an affair he now regards as over in terms of a voyage through dangerous seas safely and thankfully completed:

> ecce coronatae portum tetigere carinae,
> traiectae Syrtes, ancora iacta mihi est.

Look, my garlanded ship has reached harbour, the sandbanks
have been negotiated, my anchor has been dropped.

In a discursive situation in which love is a determining theme, the description of a journey can take on the role of a commentary on a love affair. Travel to or from, with or without, the beloved is viewed as reflecting upon the state of the relationship, as in Propertius 1.8, 1.17 or 3.21; 'separation' is conceived of in terms of geographical distance whilst erotic contentment is put in terms of staying at home, as for instance in Propertius 1.1.29–32,

> ferte per extremas gentis et ferte per undas,
> qua non ulla meum femina norit iter.
> vos remanete, quibus facili deus annuit aure,
> sitis et in tuto semper amore pares.

Take me through lands and seas at the very ends of the earth,
where no woman may know my route. But you stay put, to whom
the god assents with compliant ear, and may you ever be together
in a secure love.

The *Odyssey* provides the archetypal description of a journey the end or *telos* of which could be seen as sexual consummation, and as such explicitly informs Tibullus 1.3.[2] Many of the terms in which 'journeys' are described can bear an 'erotic' connotation as well. Thus, if the journey is through a 'cold' and 'barren' landscape, this can be seen as reflecting on the lover's sense of loneliness and unhappiness in love, and this underlies some of the most memorable treatments of love in the Western tradition, from Virgil's Gallus in the Tenth *Eclogue* through Petrarch to Schubert's *Winterreise*. So, in Propertius 1.18, the lover

---

[2] Similarly, through the eroticizing filter of elegy, the *Iliad* is regarded as a 'love' poem (cf. Prop. 2.1.13–14, *seu nuda erepto mecum luctatur amictu | tum vero longas condimus Iliadas* ('or if with clothing ripped off she wrestles naked with me, then indeed we fashion lengthy *Iliads*'); Ov. *Am.* 1.9.33–8.

represents himself in deserted places (*deserta loca*, 1) and an empty grove (*vacuum . . . nemus*, 2), places in which he is able to pour out without restraint the agonies he has kept to himself (*occultos proferre impune dolores*, 3), with the lonely rocks for confidants, if only they can keep faith (*si modo sola queant saxa tenere fidem*, 4). He catalogues the possible reasons why his Cynthia should be showing such disdain towards him, only to reject them all as false (5–18). The trees will be his witness, he proclaims (19–22), the trees which echo his words, and on whose bark he has scratched 'Cynthia'. He has learnt in fear to bear the demands of his haughty mistress (25–6), for which his reward is the cold rocks (*frigida rupes*, 27) and hard rest on a wilderness track (*inculto tramite dura quies*, 28), with the shrill birds the only audience for his complaints (29–30). But he renews his pledge of fidelity in his hope that, howsoever she is, the woods and the rocks will continue to echo 'Cynthia'.

That is one level on which this poem could be read, but there are many things that can be described in the same terms as a journey, not least the process of writing and composition. For instance, Ovid in the *Ars amatoria* constantly alludes to his progress through the poem by describing it either as a sea-voyage *en route* to port at the end of the poem (the poem rides at anchor at the end of Book 1 (772), waiting for the next stage of the journey) or as a chariot-race (e.g. 1.39–40), where the books represent the Roman equivalent of laps. The poem derives some of its piquancy from the applicability of these terms also to the sexual act. The expert's advice on how to reach simultaneous orgasm at the end of Book 2 reads:

> sed neque tu dominam velis maioribus usus
>   defice, nec cursus anteeat illa tuos;
> ad metam properate simul.

> But don't cheat your mistress by letting out your sails, nor let her
>   speed ahead of you; come together at the winning-post.   (725–7)

Ancient poets regularly represent the process of composition as wandering in groves or trackless places. 'Cynthia' can signify not only the lover's mistress, but, as the first word of Book 1, the title of the book and its primary theme as well, according to the convention whereby books were referred to by their opening words;[3] *amores* can signify not only an emotion and the person who is its object, but the title of a book of love

---

[3] Book 1 of Propertius is apparently so referred to in Mart. 14.189.

poems as well. This opens up a further dimension of possible meanings for Propertius 1.18 on the level of the poet rather than that of the lover. The poet represents himself wandering through an empty grove, places which keep silent for one *querenti* (1), complaining. The verb 'to complain' (*queri*) and the noun 'complaint' (*querella*, cf. 29) are, as we saw in relation to 1.7.8, discursively contructed as generic descriptions of writing elegy and of its subject-matter. As the lover meditates upon Cynthia's disdain, the poet reviews the potential themes that remain to him as the author of 'Cynthia'. As the lover calls to witness the trees which know something of love, and on whose bark he has scratched 'Cynthia', the poet calls to witness *si quos habet arbor amores* (19), trees which have *amores*, and he recalls *quotiens . . . scribitur . . . vestris Cynthia corticibus* (21–2), how often 'Cynthia' is written on their bark. The verb *scribere* can signify both 'to scratch' and 'to write', and *cortex* signifies the 'outer bark of a tree', corresponding to *liber*, the 'inner bark'. *liber* can in turn signify 'book'; according to the ancient Virgilian commentator Servius (on *Aeneid* 11.554), books were originally made from bark. So, 'scratching Cynthia on bark' can signify in Latin a lover scratching the name of his beloved on a tree, or a poet inscribing the theme of the mistress in a book, and here the poet calls to witness the number of times he has done this. The lover ends by re-affirming his devotion to Cynthia: in 31 he hopes that the woods will continue to echo (*resonent*) him uttering the name 'Cynthia' as he says in 21 they so often do (*resonant*). Meanwhile, in wishing for the trees to echo 'Cynthia', the poet is re-affirming his intention to continue writing on, inscribing *in libro*, (the theme of) 'Cynthia', whatever form that might take (cf. *qualiscumque es*, 31).

The commonly accepted way of talking about linguistic usages such as these is to invoke the term 'metaphor', a move I have taken great pains to avoid up to this point. The theory of metaphor has held a position of enormous authority in discussions of language stretching back to Aristotle and beyond, and it exerts considerable power over the way language is categorized and in underpinning what is deemed 'normal' in language use. In putting the question of language usage in the form 'there are words which are applicable to both journeys and love, both war and love, both journeys and arguments' and so on, I have, as a tactical ploy, rhetorically 'suspended' for the moment the distinction between literal and metaphorical. The term 'metaphor' and a distinction between 'literal' and 'metaphorical' uses of language develop with the emergence of philosophical discourse in fifth- and fourth-century Greece. Philosophy initially constituted itself as a discourse of essentializing definitions which seek out the thing-in-itself (e.g. what is justice? what is the good life?), but if its discourse was to be regarded as authoritative, it had to suggest reasons why the language it was using was more precise or more accurate than any other. One of the ways it has constantly sought to do so up to the present[4] is through the distinction between 'literal' and 'metaphorical' uses of language. All discourses seek by one means or another to control the potentiality for meaning that language has. Philosophy endeavours to restrict itself to what it defines and characterizes as primary uses of language as its way to accuracy, precision and truth, and consigns what it sees to be the secondary, the metaphorical, to other forms of discourse, notably poetry, which in collusive opposition champions the 'metaphorical' as offering superior access to truth.

The distinction between literal and metaphorical suggests that some uses of language are somehow more basic than others, that where the 'same' word can be used in two different contexts, for example love and war, one of these, the one that gets called the 'literal' use, must be in some way prior or more important; it becomes the 'normal' usage, against which all other usages of the word are 'secondary', 'figurative' or 'metaphorical'. Many would describe a phrase such as 'their relationship has *gone off the rails*' as metaphorical, thereby suggesting that it is a substitution for some literal way of describing the situation in question (say, 'their relationship has ended' or 'broken down'), that the 'proper' sphere of reference of the phrase 'gone off the rails' is train travel, and that it has been shifted across to describe the break-up of a relationship (the derivation of the Greek term *metaphora* suggesting a 'carrying across' of meaning from one distinct area to another). Historical factors are often adduced for making the distinction, on the grounds that one can understand how language works if one looks to its origins. In some respects, of course, historical and cultural factors are relevant; one doesn't talk of an affair 'going off the rails' in a world where travel by train is unknown. However, the legitimating power of the myth of origins is often invoked to determine the 'proper' sphere of reference of a word, to legislate for its usage by creating an Edenic past when language was pre-discursive, when, for example, 'conquest' unproblematically referred to, and was identical with, 'war', before the fall which wrenched signifier from signified. To say 'their relationship has gone off the rails' is not to

[4] See e.g. Habermas (1987), 185–210.

say exactly the same as 'their relationship is on the rocks', and each of these two phrases could plausibly be explicated to *mean* something different from each other, and to entail something different about the relationship than 'their relationship has ended' or 'broken down'. And are not the phrases 'has ended' and 'broken down' also applicable to descriptions of journeys and thus also metaphorical, by this definition of metaphor, when they are applied to love? This metaphorical turn is always available for repetition until language as a whole, against the philosophical *telos* underlying the distinction between 'literal' and 'metaphorical', can be represented as *essentially* metaphorical.

Fun though this deconstructive ploy can be as a formal exercise, it cannot make the distinction between 'literal' and 'metaphorical' disappear, as Derrida himself makes clear in his discussion of the 'white mythology' of metaphor.[5] In all that I have said so far, tenors of signification have been implicit: thus, if 'love can be described in terms also applicable to war', the tenor is from 'war' to 'love'. But such tenors are open to reversal; 'war' can be described in terms also applicable to 'love': nations can have *relationships*; they can *quarrel* and *fall out with* one another; military action can be described in terms which also suggest sexual potency: enemy territory (frequently anthropomorphized and gendered as female) may be *penetrated*, or defences may be *impregnable*; victories can be *conquests*. Reversing a tenor can in some cases be momentarily disconcerting. It might be objected that 'conquest' *is* (i.e. 'properly', 'really') a term of war, not love, and that its application to 'love' is somehow secondary. *Is* it? We might conceive of the issues in terms of identity, that which constitutes 'the self' or 'the thing itself' over against 'the other'. Do you like something enough to feel a sense of relationship, to 'identify' with it? The impossibility of *total* identity ('sameness') with something else simultaneously creates a sense of difference or of disliking. One's self-sufficiency, one's autonomy, is both constituted and at the same time put into question by a sense of liking/disliking; one feels the lack of, or desire for, what one 'is' not, what one does not have, that which is missing from being 'whole', from being a totality with existence. This 'love/hate' is a way of expressing the relationship between the 'self' (I/we/this) and the 'other' (you/them/that). As we saw in the previous chapter, the use of any term involves the simultaneous projection of 'sameness' and 'difference': if something is 'like', sameness is asserted, but not total identity – that is, difference is

[5] Derrida (1982), 207–71.

also asserted. *Odi et amo* are inextricably entangled with each other, and 'love/hate' and the constellation of terms involved are therefore, arguably *par excellence*, what Lakoff and Johnson[6] call a 'metaphor we live by' – in this case the means by which we image, structure and articulate notions of *relationship*, applicable in whatever 'area' such notions are expressed. Thus for example one can *like* or *dislike* a particular text, striving to master it, making it articulate one's identity. Thus it is once again possible to envisage how Ovid's question to Cupid ('*an, quod ubique, tuum est?*') could be answered in the affirmative.

The question then arises: not is there, but could there ever be, a set of terms whose exclusive or 'proper' function is to describe love? Can there be a 'literal' language of love, which describes the thing-in-itself? Not from this 'anti-essentializing' perspective within which 'identity' is constituted by the simultaneous projection of 'sameness' and 'difference', and hence where there are no autonomous, pre-discursive, basic 'areas' from which meaning can be 'carried across' to new ones. Language is, however, never just a *system*, disconnected from use in context. 'In practice' then (though 'theory' and 'practice' exist in a collusive relationship), in the contestation of discursive meaning out of which language is constituted, people attempt to 'fix' a particular usage *as* 'reality', render it the 'proper', 'natural', 'obvious', 'real' or 'true' application of a term, and terminology thus becomes concretized into 'autonomous' areas or fields, in one of which its use will be deemed 'literal'. Language in use always encodes values and assumptions about what is important and what is not, and distinctions between what is regarded as a 'literal' use of language and what is regarded as a 'metaphorical' use, as soon as they move away from the realm of the theoretical to invoke a specific example, reveal the influence of quite specific ideological values and assumptions in the construction and manipulation of the distinction. Indeed, the very distinction that is drawn between the 'literal' and 'metaphorical' uses of a word provides, by virtue of being largely unquestioned, a framework within which a hierarchy of values and assumptions can be articulated.

Thus when distinctions are drawn about words such as 'conquest' or 'surrender', and their 'proper' or 'literal' sphere is deemed to be that of 'warfare' whilst their application to instances of 'love' is deemed 'figurative' or 'metaphorical', it reveals that what is being said about

---

[6] Lakoff and Johnson (1980).

'warfare' and 'love' exists in a complex and interrelated hierarchy of values which manifests itself in unexpected ways, as in the division between literal and metaphorical. If the distinction drawn seems 'natural' or 'proper', it can say something about the way one is accommodated to the dominant ideological assumptions of society and to the hierarchies of power and the institutions these assumptions inform.[7] On yet another level, it articulates society's prevailing assumptions about what it terms 'love'. The surprise so often expressed that love should be described in terms also used for war, a surprise that manifests itself by calling this use metaphorical, is indicative of a definition of love which wishes to exclude or disown notions of violence, aggression, the desire to impose domination or to have domination imposed, to exclude the '*odi*' within '*amo*', and the texts of elegy can be read in such a way as to suppress or emphasize such notions in the service of differing ideological projections of 'love'. Violence figures in elegiac erotic scenes, so much so in the reading of Paul Veyne that he is moved to speak in passing of 'sadism'.[8] For example in *Am.* 1.5, when Corinna comes to make love in the noon-day heat, the lover rips off her tunic while she fights to remain covered by it (*deripui tunicam . . .|pugnabat tunica sed tamen illa tegi*, 13–14). Fights or 'fights'? It is precisely in the ambiguity within the word, between – is it to be called 'collusion' or 'resistance', 'consent' or 'refusal', 'desire' or 'repugnance'? – that the (male) *magister amoris* locates the politics of sexual relations, and he 'resolves' the issue by legislating for the 'real' meaning of the term *vis*:

> vim licet appelles: grata est vis ista puellis;
> quod iuvat, invitae saepe dedisse volunt.   (*Ars* 1.673–4)

You are permitted to apply force: that sort of force is pleasing to girls; often, what gives them pleasure, unwillingly they are willing to yield.

The range of application of the Latin verb *appellare* permits another translation of line 673: 'though you may call it "force", that sort of "force" is pleasing to girls'. There are numerous references in elegy to the

---

[7] Genre could be taken as one such naturalizing institution, helping to determine what is read as a literal and what as a metaphorical field of reference in any particular context. Thus epic is 'about war', and so 'war' is described in 'metaphors' from other 'fields', whilst elegy is 'about love', with 'love' being described in 'metaphors' from other 'fields'.   [8] Veyne (1988), 225 n.5.

excitement engendered (sic?) by the *rixa*, the physical erotic brawl, and the pleasure of physical domination, for example in Tibullus 1.10.53–66, especially 59–66, where the 'legitimate' limits of violence are ratified, and the distinction between *vis* in 'love' and in 'war' ordained:

> A lapis est ferrumque, suam quicumque puellam
> verberat: e caelo deripit ille deos.
> sit satis e membris tenuem rescindere vestem,
> sit satis ornatus dissoluisse comae,
> sit lacrimas movisse satis. quater ille beatus
> quo tenera irato flere puella potest.
> sed manibus qui saevus erit, scutumque sudemque
> is gerat et miti sit procul a Venere.

Ah, that man is stone and steel who beats his girl: he drags the gods down from heaven. Let it be sufficient to tear the thin clothes from her limbs; let it be sufficient to disturb the arrangement of her hair; and to excite tears. Four times blest is he at whose anger his tender girl can weep. But the one who is going to be savage with his hands should take up his shield and stake and get far away from gentle Venus.

Ovid, *Amores* 1.7 presents a dramatized scene of the lover's remorse at having struck his girl, but it is a remorse undercut by the excitement he expresses at the effect of his blows – the attractiveness of her dishevelled hair (11–12) and her combination of fear and hostility towards him (20–1); sexual violence, he ponders, should be restricted to love bites (41–2). Her tears move him to feel guilt, but again this is undercut by his observation as he falls at her feet that she shrinks back from the hands she has come to fear (61–2). The elegiac lover's self-styled 'enslavement' to his mistress needs to be seen in the light of this pleasure in sexual aggression and domination, a theme to be resumed in the next chapter, as will be the identification of *vis* with physical violence.

The relationship between 'areas' which have terms in common is always open to ideological representation. For example, a verb frequently used in Victorian times for experiencing an orgasm was 'to spend'. An influential recent book on modern ideas of sexuality by Stephen Heath, *The Sexual Fix*,[9] would have us see this term as a link between what is

---

[9] Heath (1982).

often represented as the Victorian obsession with prostitution and the Victorian virtue of thrift, thus suggesting that sexual and financial continence were intertwined in Victorian ideology. A thought-provoking idea and a way into analysing ideologies, but not a cut-and-dried answer to what Victorian society was 'really' like, for 'Victorian values', what they were and their relevance to the present day, are a focal point for a contemporary ideological struggle of which Heath's book is itself a part. Elegy describes 'love' in terms also used to describe 'war' in a society frequently represented these days as obsessed with militarism, and thus raises similarly open-ended questions of ideological analysis which have been much discussed in recent work.[10] I stress open-ended, for elegy is always open – inevitably open – to appropriation to represent ideological positions in the present, the more persuasive of which will succeed temporarily in imposing their rhetoric of reality and truth. Inscribed in this rhetoric is the theory of metaphor itself which provides a seemingly objective rationale for privileging certain terms like 'conquest' as *really* describing 'war' rather than 'love' or *vice versa*. However, a tenor of signification can always be emphasized or reversed within a particular ideological framework in pursuit of a particular end, as we saw the contemporary discourse of sexuality plots a tenor *from* 'sex' *to* 'politics' and reads its texts accordingly.

It is also possible to draw attention, as I did at the start of this chapter, to the way that one thing can be systematically presented in a range of terms 'habitually' associated with some other thing. Ovid does this with the terminology common to 'love' and 'warfare' in *Amores* 1.9. The piquancy depends on the degree to which the 'two' domains of signification which share common terms are perceived as separate or even antithetical to each other, as, to pick an instance at random, between 'sex' and 'scholarship', a distinction which people spend exhaustive efforts in maintaining. There are considerable social and institutional constraints which work to suppress within particular discursive contexts awareness of the applicability also to sex of terms central in those contexts, just as there are constraints on the contexts, and the terms, in which sex can be mentioned. These constraints can, however, be circumvented by using words which adequately describe one thing, but have the capacity to be used of sex as well. Comedy thrives on

---

[10] See e.g. Myerowitz (1985), 62–72; Gamel (1989), arguing that Latin usage suggests a continuum between male sexual and military aggression.

this capacity. Take for example this joke by the music hall comedian Max Miller, which exploits, amongst others, the ambiguity of terms which can refer to journeys and to sex. Max meets a ravishing blonde on a narrow mountain path and debates furiously with himself: 'do I block her passage or toss myself off?' Roman elegy is a highly formalized mode of writing which observes some restraints on its diction. For example, anatomical terms are rare, even in Ovid's poem on impotence (*Amores* 3.7), in which the discursive contraints are simultaneously observed and highlighted by the enormous lengths the poet goes to so as to fall in with convention and avoid calling the sitting member by name. The *Amores* constantly flirt with the potentiality of some extremely common Latin words to have a sexual reference. Thus in *Amores* 1.9.21ff., the poet discourses on the value of night assaults for the soldier. No less so for adulterous lovers who take advantage of the sleep of husbands and 'brandish their weapons while the enemy sleep' (*et sua sopitis hostibus arma movent*, 26). *arma* can refer to 'weapons', but it also a colloquial term for 'penis'.[11]

To press this point further, let us turn to the first poem of the first book of Ovid's *Amores*. Opening poems occupy a vital position in a poetic collection, and the convention whereby books are referred to by their first words makes opening lines particularly crucial. Propertius' first book seems to have been referred to as his 'Cynthia', as we have seen, and that opening word encapsulates the theme of the book, the pre-eminence of the mistress. In the generation or so before Ovid was writing, the poetic theme whereby the poet announced his intention to write an elevated sort of verse, such as epic, but was prevented by the intervention of the god of poetry, had become widespread following Virgil's imitation of Callimachus' prologue to the *Aetia* at the start of his Sixth *Eclogue*. *Amores* 1.1. sends up all these conventions. The poet presents himself as preparing to write an epic until the intervention of Cupid – to the outrage of the poet not even the god of poetry – stops him. The poem even starts as though it is going to be an epic. Its first word, *arma*, proclaims the theme of war, and if this poem was written in the aftermath of the publication of Virgil's *Aeneid*, it may even have been alluding to the poem which was itself well known by its opening words, *arma virumque cano*, 'arms and the man I sing'. Epics are conventionally written in hexameter verse, and, as composition can be figured in terms also applicable to journeying, Cupid effectively trips up the poet by pulling one of his feet

[11] See Adams (1982), 21.

out from under him (*unum surripuisse pedem*, 4; *pes* is applicable to both the foot you stand on and a metrical foot), thus turning his hexameters, the metre 'appropriate to' epic subject-matter (*materia conveniente modis*, 2) into elegiac couplets, the metre 'appropriate to' love elegy (*materia . . . numeris levioribus apta*, 19). So, the opening word of the poem is a false start. Having set out to write *arma*, epic, the poet finds himself only able to write elegiac couplets. Or is it a false start? The theme of the mistress is not central to the *Amores* in the way that it is to Propertius 1, but the themes of *arma*, the male equipment, and *violenta . . . bella*, i.e. *rixae*, arguably are. In the last chapter we saw how Propertius 1.7 could be read in such a way as to suggest that genres of writing are gendered; epic there was *durus*, with associations of 'masculinity', whilst elegy's designation as *mollis* suggested 'effeminacy'. The elegiac couplet mimics epic in that its first line is a hexameter of six metrical feet (referred to here in line 2 as *gravi numero*, 'in a heavy beat'), but then its second line trails off in five (cf. *numeris levioribus*, 'in lighter measures', 19). By a careful choice of terms in 17–18, the poet speaks of the elegiac couplet in such a way as to suggest the erection and detumescence of the penis:

> cum bene surrexit versu nova pagina primo,
> attenuat nervos proximus ille meos

'When my new page *has risen up* well with its first verse, the next verse diminishes my – *nervos*'. The word *nervus* can refer to a sinew, muscle, strength, literary vigour[12] – and the penis. It can also refer to the string of a bow, and 'stringing your bow' seems to be a colloquial way in Latin of saying 'have an erection';[13] *attenuare* is found elsewhere of the 'weakening effects of love'.[14] In 17–18, the suggestion is only a fleeting one, but in case we missed it, we are given another opportunity in 27:

> sex mihi surgat opus numeris, in quinque residat

Let my *opus* rise in six feet, and sink back in five

opus can mean a literary work but it can also mean 'sexual intercourse' and 'the penis'.[15] It is the term which both describes the *Amores* and gives

---

[12] See Brink (1971), 110.   [13] See Adams (1982), 21.

[14] McKeown (1989), 22 ad loc.

[15] See Adams (1982), 57, where the sexual connotations of *surgere* are also discussed. For the sexual connotations of *numerus* cf. *Am.* 3.7.26, *me memini numeros sustinuisse novem*, 'I remember I managed it nine times'.

59

the work its characteristic structure and thrust. In *Am.* 2.10.35–8., the lover utters a prayer:

> at mihi contingat Veneris languescere motu,
>   cum moriar, medium solvar et inter opus;
> atque aliquis nostro lacrimans in funere dicat
>   'conveniens vitae mors fuit ista tuae.'

But when I die, may it be my good fortune to come to it in Venus' uprising, and may I find release right in the middle of the job;[16] and let some mourner at my funeral say 'that was a fitting climax to your life'.

This reference to 'dying' *medium . . . inter opus* itself comes in a poem that, at the very middle of Book 2, stands *medium . . . inter opus*. The collection ends with an assertion, by now a convention in poetry of the time, that the *Amores* will assure for their author a sort of life after death:

> inbelles elegi, genialis Musa, valete,
>   post mea mansurum fata superstes opus.   (3.15.19–20)

Peaceable elegies, Muse close to my heart, farewell, a piece destined to remain standing long after I've come and gone.

With the postponement of *opus* until the very end, Ovid administers a turn to the final screw in the coffin of an exhausted topos. Similarly, the *Ars amatoria*, which describes the techniques of sexual seduction, structures itself in terms of the sexual act. As the work achieves its *telos* in the description of simultaneous orgasm (2.719–32), the poet can at last proclaim at the climax: *finis adest operi*, 'that's the end of the job'.

Ovid's latest commentator remarks *à propos* the possible sexual innuendo in the description of metres in *Amores* 1.1.17–18: 'since . . . Ovid emphasizes in the next couplet that he has no beloved, such an undertone does not seem appropriate here.'[17] In seeking to ground the 'objective' meaning of the text which is the commentator's goal, the term 'appropriate' presents itself as a criterion of universal validity, imposing a reassuring closure on further explication precisely when the contingencies of meaning are at their most fluid. The term can be invoked when the

---

[16] For *solvere* connoting death cf. e.g. Hor. *Ep.* 1.16.78, and orgasm cf. e.g. Virg. *Geo.* 4.199; on 'dying' as a term for orgasm, see generally Adams (1982), 159.

[17] McKeown (1989), 22.

text has been most thoroughly *appropriated* within and by a particular ideological framework so as to instantiate its assumptions of 'propriety', assumptions which work to police the demarcation of category distinctions of 'autonomous' areas. It is, of course, demonstrably inappropriate that the stateliest measure ever moulded by the lips of man, and its wielder, should even by the remotest implication be made the object of a crude sexual innuendo, and arguments can always be devised to prove that the sense is not 'there'. But notions of 'propriety' and 'appropriateness' constitute and in turn are shaped by the possibility of 'impropriety' and 'inappropriateness', and seek to deny 'reality' to improper or inappropriate uses of language along with their legitimacy.[18] Like the jokes of Max Miller, *Amores* 1.1 seems to offer the possibility of being read 'innocently', only to cast doubt on the possibility of an 'innocent' reading. Indeed, it constantly appeals to the criterion of 'propriety' only to render that criterion problematic by the very terms in which the appeal is made. The signifying potentiality of language constantly escapes the poet's attempts to use it 'properly'. The poet recounts how he was starting to write an epic 'with subject-matter appropriate to the metre' (*materia conveniente modis*, 2), when Cupid stole one foot from under him and left him with an elegiac couplet. But at a second glance, what the poet says he was writing about, *arma* and *violenta . . . bella* (1), the *militia amoris*, turn out after all to be the subject-matter appropriate to the elegiac couplet, and the slipperiness of the criterion of propriety is rendered graphic by the terms in which it is depicted, for *modi*, as well as being applicable to metres, is also a term for the various sexual positions couples can adopt.[19] Furthermore, the verb indicating appropriateness (*convenire*) is one of the most polite of euphemisms for the sexual act.[20] Thus the *materia* already adumbrated in line 1 does indeed come together in a nice 'fit' in the term *modis*.

A second opportunity for readers to take the point is given in the poet's final protestations to Cupid in 19–20 (*nec mihi materia est numeris levioribus apta,|aut puer aut longas compta puella comas*), where similar sorts of play are made on the terms *numeris* and *apta*. But the very verb he uses to refer to his protestations, *questus eram* (21), serves to undermine them, as it depicts him as already doing what he says he can't do, write

---

[18] This point comes, apropriat(iv)ely, from John Henderson.

[19] See Adams (1982), 177, who notes it as the Latin equivalent of the Greek term *schēmata*; *figura* is similarly applicable to sexual position, cf. e.g. Ov. *Ars* 2.679, 3.772, *Rem.* 407, *Tr.* 2.523.   [20] See Adams (1982), 179.

elegy, and Cupid is about to drive the point home in no uncertain terms. As he stretches his bow, he says '*quod . . . canas, vates, accipe . . . opus*' (24), which could be read as 'take this, bard, as a subject for your poems'.[21] The text could equally be construed to mean 'as something that you can sing of, bard, take – *opus*.[22] Cupid gives the poet both his literary task and his subject-matter, sex, in one word. And possibly even more than that.[23] The poet's desire to see the world in neat categorical distinctions is made clear in lines 7–12 in the course of his argument that each of the gods has a clearly demarcated sphere of activity. He has made his anxieties about different *modi* and what is appropriate to them abundantly clear; line 28 once again asserts that each genre has its appropriate *modi*. Cupid's bow is already tightly strung (apparently very tightly, cf. 23) and in the words *accipe . . . opus* he ensures that the poet is receptive, thus graphically figuring the passive role which is incorporated in elegy's own representation of itself as *mollis*.[24] McKeown's character-ization of the poet as 'the impotent victim of the deity's interference'[25] seems entirely appropriate. The poet had earlier enquired of Cupid *cur opus adfectas ambitiose novum*? ('why do you aspire in your ambition to a further undertaking?', 14),[26] ostensibly innocent of the possible signifi-cance of his words. By the opening poem of Book 3, the poet is more worldly-wise about his role and knows the score. Confronted with the competing attentions of Elegy and Tragedy, who, though both female, show very divergent gender characteristics,[27] he encourages his *Amores* to get on with it while the way is clear (*teneri properentur Amores,|dum vacat*), for *a tergo grandius urguet opus* ('a bigger piece is pressing hard in my rear', 3.1.69–70).

The language of literary, grammatical and rhetorical analysis is also the language of sexual position.[28] The very language of figuration has sex

---

[21] Barsby (1973), 42.

[22] For a similarly pointed postponement of *opus* cf. *Ars* 3.770. McKeown (1989, 26, ad loc.) notes that 'Ovid uses the form *opus* 186 times in his elegiac poetry, 114 times in this position'.

[23] I am grateful to Catharine Edwards for pointing me in this direction.

[24] *accipe* was frequently inscribed on missiles (McKeown (1989), 26), with overt sexual innuendo; cf. the inscriptions on the significantly named *Perusinae glandes* discussed by Hallett (1977). It is also a term used in one of the most famous scenes of poetic initiation, that of Gallus in Virgil's Sixth *Eclogue* (69): *hos tibi dant calamos (en accipe) Musae* ('the Muses gives these reeds to you (here, have them)').

[25] McKeown (1989), 10.   [26] Trans. Barsby (1973), 40–2.

[27] Wyke (1989b), 117–34.   [28] Cf. Adams (1982), 179–80.

embedded within it, and it can always be 'troped', turned round the other way. *Amores* I.I can serve as a reminder that, where tenors of signification are concerned, you can have it either way (or both, if you wish), and the poem offers the frisson of finding out what terms of literary analysis feel like when experienced *a posteriori*. This will seem to some a perverse position to adopt, but they should recall that meaning is only fully realized at the point of reception. That at any rate is the gist of Ovid's self-defence from exile against the charge, the mode of reading, that would impute all responsibility for meaning to the author. Those who would seek to deny the play of signification within a text and its capacity for reconfiguration by readers run the risk of exposing only themselves. *Amores* I.I denies to those floundering in a sea of signification an appeal to 'grounds' by depriving them even of what they always assumed to be the reassuring sense of 'touching bottom'.

CHAPTER

4

A lover's discourse

In 'The Hitchhiking Game', the first of the short stories that make up Milan Kundera's *Laughable Loves*,[1] a travelling couple on impulse adopt, but then become entangled in, the roles of female hitchhiker and the driver who picks her up. Their relationship undergoes a dramatic change as their sense of what they and their partner 'really' are becomes a function of their new roles, and they are led to question whether their previous identities, their previous 'selves', were no less founded upon a set of roles. Pushed to the extreme as a way of exploring the essence of an individual, this approach can only reveal that one's individuality consists *essentially* in role-playing: Kundera's story ends with its heroine repeatedly sobbing in psychological torment 'I am me'. To romantic notions of the individual, which see in expressions of love the ultimate definition of the self, the phrase 'I love you' represents a climactic moment of truth, and so its use is hedged around with hesitations, expectations, hopes, dreams and anxieties. The moment of using the phrase can be one of exhilaration, but it can also, particularly in retrospect, seem a disappointment. One reaction, particularly for those who have internalized the ideology of romantic love, is that this cannot have been the moment of truth after all, and to resume, perhaps repeatedly, the search for an object of love that will fulfil all needs and desires and bring the longed-for sense of wholeness. From such a perspective, it is disconcerting to feel that the phrase 'I love you' may have emerged from our mouths already equipped with inverted commas, that we may have been acting out a script that has been played out, with much the same plot and much the same words, by many before us, that

[1] Kundera (1975), 1–25.

what we say and feel in love may not be unique to each of us, but moulded and refined by many before us. La Rochefoucauld's maxim can bear another repetition: 'Some people would never have been in love, had they never heard love talked about.' Or to put this in the terms suggested by Roland Barthes, there is a lover's discourse and we construct ourselves as amorous subjects within it; thus 'no love is original'.[2] In treating love as a *system* which can be taught and learned, Ovid's *Ars amatoria* similarly views it as a discursive artefact. The phrase *tu mihi sola places* ('you are the only one for me') functions as an expression of the lover's exclusive devotion to the beloved (e.g. Propertius 2.7.19). In prefixing to it the words '*elige cui dicas*' ('choose to whom you may say', *Ars* 1.42), the *magister amoris* makes of it a script to be performed. Within this way of viewing things, to be in love is to think one's self 'in love' and 'act' accordingly.

These two positions are ostensibly opposites, and are often represented as such in the discourse of Roman elegy, with the opening poems of the Propertian and Ovidian collections being taken as projecting the different perspectives. The opening words of Propertius 1.1, 'Cynthia first captured wretched me with her eyes', thus encapsulate the myth of love at first sight, with the lover the powerless victim of a force beyond his control (*Amor*, personified as a deity, tramples him underfoot in a gesture of triumph, 3–4), a force embodied in, and identified with, the beloved, and subjectively experienced in terms of illness (cf. *contactum*, 2) and madness (cf. *furor*, 7), which disrupts all efforts, indeed even the desire, to live a 'normal' life which observes accepted social conventions (cf. *donec me docuit castas odisse puellas|improbus, et nullo vivere consilio*, 5–6). In the first poem of Ovid's *Amores*, the poet finds himself obliged to write elegy even though he has no boy or girl to write about (20); the assumption that one writes love poetry *because* one has fallen in love with somebody comes under question. In the second poem, the narrator represents himself in bed, suffering extreme symptoms of restlessness (1–4), and pondering to himself what he is to say that these are (the essentializing verb *par excellence*, *esse*, heads the poem). They could easily be construed as the symptoms of 'love', but the narrator seems to nip this speculation in the bud: 'I'd know it, I suppose, if I were the victim of some love's attack' (*nam, puto, sentirem, si quo temptarer amore*, 5). But though they have no obvious cause in his case, these are the

[2] Barthes (1979), 136.

recognized symptoms of love, and since he also knows that the assaults of love are not always frontal (6), the discursive pressures drive him towards the conclusion: 'that will be it' (*sic erit*, 7). Already the question has been raised whether one can be in love without an object for that love. Now comes the further question: is 'to be in love' not necessarily to be in love with somebody, but to think one's self in love, to adopt the subject position within the lover's discourse, to take on and act out the role of the lover? The agonized self-examination which provides the structuring theme for Virgil's Gallus in the Tenth *Eclogue*, for the Delia, Marathus and Nemesis poems of Tibullus, and for the whole of Propertius' first book and beyond, the struggle for understanding which 'is' the lover's discourse,[3] lasts for precisely one line: 'do I yield, or do I feed the sudden fire by struggling against it?' (*cedimus, an subitum luctando accendimus ignem*?, 9), and submission comes in a single word, *cedamus* (10), 'let's yield'.

The position represented as 'Ovidian' is surprising only insofar as the one represented as 'Propertian' is assumed to speak the truth about love. And *vice versa*, of course, for 'Propertius' is always open to a recuperative reading from the point of view of 'Ovid' as a dramatic mimesis of the lover's discourse. Roland Barthes's contemporary 'ars amatoria', ambiguous in its sexuality, arbitrary to the extent of organizing its constituent categories in alphabetical order, slides between systemization and dramatic mimesis of a lover's discourse. This technique, and the English title of the work, which talks of *fragments* of *a* lover's discourse, serve rhetorically to distance it from, though they cannot evade, the universalizing pretensions of the analysis and the ('romantic') categories within which, however critically, it is framed. The French title (*Fragments d'un discours amoreux*) avoids reference to a *lover*. Nonetheless, the discourse's 'voice' or 'subject', whether it be Barthes's bisexual lover or the male 'heterosexual' elegiac lover (de)constructed in this book, is open to reading as normative (and thus as marginalizing other voices and sexual ideologies). Furthermore, description *as* a discourse (especially if underpinned by the definite article) serves rhetorically to create an impression of objectivity, the apparent possibility of adopting a position 'outside' the discourse and its effects from which it can be adequately

---

[3] Barthes characterizes the issue the lover endlessly mulls over as 'not: *make it stop!* but: *I want to understand* (what is happening to me)!' (1979, 60). The sense of a structure or system, from the seemingly secure categories of which he feels excluded, is in Barthes's scheme a constitutive feature of the lover's discourse (1979, 45–7).

described or criticized, the illusion of total control, a view that the Ovidian *magister amoris* of course cultivates but also undermines.[4] If love can be viewed, and reflected upon, as a discursive artefact, it is also a discourse which we inhabit, a discourse which 'works' its 'effects' insofar as it is internalized and reproduced as a 'spontaneous' or 'natural' expression of behaviour. But such formulations, however disinterested they may seem in their presentation, never escape service to some end or other. The *magister amoris* once more:

> est tibi agendus amans imitandaque vulnera verbis;
>   haec tibi quaeratur qualibet arte fides.
> nec credi labor est: sibi quaeque videtur amanda;
>   pessima sit, nulli non sua forma placet.
> saepe tamen vere coepit simulator amare;
>   saepe, quod incipiens finxerat esse, fuit.   (*Ars* 1.611–16)

You must play the part of the lover and mimic the wounds of love in your words; you are to win her belief by whatever means it takes. That's no great task – every woman seems to her own eyes a natural object of passion; however awful she may be, there is none to whom her own appearance is not a source of satisfaction. Often, however, he who feigns begins to love in reality; often he becomes in fact what he had started by pretending to be.

At what point can 'feigned' love be said to have become 'real'? Such analyses tend to blur any distinction between 'real' and 'false', but the rhetoric of reality is nonetheless retained to invite the collusion of females in their own seduction:

> (quo magis, o, faciles imitantibus este puellae:
>   fiet amor verus, qui modo falsus erat.)   (1.617–18)

(So you should be all the more indulgent, girls, to those who feign: the love which started by being false will turn out to be true.)

Treating the language of love as discourse can serve to reveal the rhetoricity that such language so often succeeds in occluding, not least from those who are involved in it. By prefacing the words *tu mihi sola places* with the instruction *elige cui dicas*, the *magister amoris* treats them as re-usable, suggesting an element of tactical choice and calculation in

---

[4] Cf. e.g. *Ars* 2.547–8; also *Am.* 2.18.20.

the use of a phrase of ostensibly exclusive applicability. *Amores* 1.3 offers a dramatic mimesis of the situation, an apparent declaration of eternal and exclusive fidelity to a particular individual:

> non mihi *mille placent*, non sum desultor amoris:
> tu mihi, si qua fides, cura perennis eris;
> tecum, quos dederint annos mihi fila sororum,
> vivere contingat teque dolente mori. (15–18)

I don't tell a *thousand* girls that they are *the one for me*, I don't leap from one love to the next: believe me, you will be my everlasting passion. May it be my fate to live with you for whatever years the sisters' threads grant to me, and to die with you there lamenting me.

The lover presents himself as in the power of his addressee, who has, he says, made him her prey (cf. *praedata . . . est*, 1) and to whom he is prepared to be a slave through the long years (cf. *deserviat*, 5), and as one who knows how to love with absolute fidelity (*pura . . . fide*, 6). The lover requests of her that she make herself available as a subject for his poetry, promising that poems will result that are worthy of their source of inspiration (19–20). However, the lover's invocation of three mythological heroines (Io, Leda and Europa, 21–4) to illustrate the fame that poetry can confer serves to identify him with the single figure who seduced all three, the archetypal adulterer Jupiter, thus casting doubt on the 'sincerity' of his earlier protestations. But also perhaps on the unexamined notions of *fides* or 'sincerity' themselves, the rhetoric of the declaration *tu mihi sola places*. What is it about 'you' that makes 'you' uniquely attractive? *Amores* 2.10 explores the possibility of being 'in love' with two women at the same time: the lover is attracted to both, and can't make up his mind which is the more attractive, the one to whom he might say *tu mihi sola places*:

> pulchrior hac illa est, haec est quoque pulchrior illa,
> et magis haec nobis et magis illa *placet*. (7–8)

That one is more beautiful than this one . . . and yet this one is more beautiful than that one . . . this one *is more the one* for me . . . and yet that one is.

What if 'you' are not an essence, but the possessor of attractive 'features'? In 2.4.9–10, the lover protests that there is not one particular type of appearance that attracts his attention; there are a hundred reasons why he should always be in love:

> non est certa meos quae forma invitet amores:
> centum sunt causae cur ego semper amem.

'In love' with what? *amem* has no object here, and the poem takes on the form of a catalogue of female *attributes*. Can love be exclusive if its object is an amalgam of culturally constructed, and hence transferred and transferrable, qualities? Does the 'unique' object of love 'play the role' of all the (wo)men a (wo)man can be for the lover? Is *amores*, the word the lover uses to describe his desire (9), the word that can denote the object of that desire, the girl-friend, the word that also denotes the collection of poems that Ovid writes, 'singular' or 'plural'? Is the possibility of being in love with one only possible within the context of the possibility of being in love with many? Elegy's self-description as a *fallax opus* (Propertius 4.1.135) raises the question of whether 'deceit' – of either the beloved or the lover who makes it or both – is always at some level a part of a 'sincere' profession of love. As a corollary to this, the presentation of elegy in terms of 'sincerity' or 'whole love' plays a rhetorically analogous role in the relationship of critic and reader. *Amores* 1.3 ends with the lover promising that he and his beloved will be celebrated throughout the whole world, and his name will always be linked with hers (*nos quoque per totum pariter cantabimur orbem|iunctaque semper erunt nomina nostra tuis*, 25–6). But what is her name? The name 'Corinna' does not figure before 1.5. The poem is an all-purpose declaration to any girl who is prepared to perform the actions designated by the verb *amare* (2, 3). All willing should fill in their names in the blank space.

The issue of identity, what a person or thing *is*, is posed and explored in the question of relationship, for which a physical or emotional relationship with another person, and the language of 'desire' and 'possession' in which it is articulated, provide a paradigm instance. In embodying a sense of 'otherness', the beloved seems to offer the prospect of a wholeness in the fulfilment of every 'lack' that the lover as a consequence feels 'within' himself or herself. The notion of total mutuality, the idea of two lovers fusing into a single whole being, is one of the most characteristic expressions of lovers' discourse. In Plato's *Symposium* (189C–193E), Aristophanes tells the myth of the round people. Originally humans were round and whole until they were sliced in two by Zeus to punish their presumption. Since then, sensing that they were once whole, they have spent their lives searching for their missing halves. The desire to be 'one' with the loved object is explored in Ovid's story of Narcissus (*Met.* 3.402ff.). Having spurned the attentions of Echo and the nymphs, he is cursed by one of them:

> sic amet ipse licet, sic non potiatur amato! (405)

Thus may he himself love, thus may he not possess what he loves!

For him to possess what he loves, what he loves must be other than himself.[5] Narcissus falls in love with his own reflection in a pool and both does and cannot achieve this 'oneness' with the object of his desire. He courts his own image in the kind of language lovers habitually use – lamenting separation and the obstacles, however tiny, which keep them apart (442ff.) – until he realises that he 'is' what he loves (463). Narcissus achieves what lovers often crave, total identity with the object of his love. And his first wish when he realises this (467–8)?

> o utinam a nostro secedere corpore possem!
> votum in amante novum, vellem, quod amamus abesset!

Oh that I could be parted from my own body! A novel prayer for a lover, I wish that what I love were absent from me!

He wishes for separateness from what he loves, for it is only in that separateness that the question of relationship, expressed in terms of 'love' and the 'desire to possess', can be articulated. Identity is constituted in the interplay of 'sameness' and 'difference', the 'difference' *within* 'sameness' and the 'sameness' *within* 'difference'.

The notion of possession which informs the nymph's curse (and the common elegiac idiom *habere*, to 'have') works to construe the beloved as a thing. Barthes repeatedly uses the phrase 'the loved object' in describing the way in which the beloved's autonomy of feeling or action becomes in a lover's discourse of secondary importance to the motives or actions attributed to him or her by the lover, to the extent that the beloved is depersonalized and becomes an object. 'But isn't desire always the same, whether the object is present or absent? Isn't the object *always* absent?' he remarks.[6] Even if the object of the desire to possess is physically present,

---

[5] Ovid elsewhere (*Fasti* 5.226) addresses Narcissus as *infelix, quod non alter et alter eras*, 'unhappy in that you were not two people at the same time'.

[6] Barthes (1979), 15.

its absence is *staged* in the lover's discourse.[7] In Propertius 1.2, the lover
criticizes the beloved for wearing make-up and expensive clothes (1–4).
Unadorned, 'natural' beauty is more pleasing to the lover (5–14), a theme
which recurs in 2.18 and Tibullus 1.8. 'Nature' in this context is
constructed by the lover in terms of landscape features – flowers, plants,
water, coloured pebbles, and birds which sing more sweetly *nulla ... arte*,
with the aid of no contrivance (14), thus engineering a distinction
between 'nature' and 'culture' and 'grounding' his discourse within the
former. *Amores* 1.14 places the Ovidian lover in a dramatic situation
which is a disastrous extension of this theme: as a result of dyeing, the
beloved's hair has just fallen out, and she sits before the lover holding her
hair in her lap. Though the poem is a representation of a dramatic
situation, it consists entirely of the lover's monologue, and we apprehend
the situation, and perceive the beloved and her reactions, only through
the lover's words and the perspectives they assert. Faced with the
situation described in line 2, that the beloved's hair has fallen out, the
lover's first reaction is to interpret the situation as a vindication of
himself, the opening word of the poem incorporating the first person
singular (1):

Dicebam 'medicare tuos desiste capillos'

I kept on telling you 'Stop dyeing your hair'

The use of the imperfect tense in *dicebam*, 'I kept on telling you', suggests
a repeated scene in the past, comparable to that of Propertius 1.2. We are
supplied with a 'history' for this relationship in the lover's words, and like
every 'history', it incorporates a *telos* and is moulded in terms of the
concerns of the perspective it offers. Why does the lover wish to stop his
beloved dyeing her hair, for he is prepared to admit in passing that it was
suited to a hundred styles (*centum flexibus apti*, 13)? The Propertian lover
makes much of preferring what he terms 'natural' beauty, but there is
more involved in his statement than the simple expression of an aesthetic
preference. The lover expresses his sense of himself by means of an
endless series of identifications: lovers scrutinize every amorous system
they come across and try to discern what place they would have in that
system were they part of it. Herein lies one of the chief functions of myth

---

[7] Cf. Barthes (1979), 13 on 'absence': 'Any episode of language which stages the
absence of the loved object – whatever its cause and its duration – and which tends to
transform this absence into an ordeal of abandonment.' Thus love is often described
in terms also applicable to journeys.

in Propertian elegy. In the first poem of Book 1, the lover recounts his enslavement to Cynthia in lines 1–8. In line 9, without more ado, the story of Milanion and Atalanta is recounted. As Barthes observes,[8] what lovers perceive are not simply analogies, but homologies: the relationship is a structural one – I am (or am not) to Cynthia what Milanion was to Atalanta. To the extent that the lover feels alienated from the 'reality' he assumes the rest of the world to be experiencing, and from which he feels himself excluded,[9] he feels a powerful sense of identification with anyone he perceives as experiencing similar feelings to his own, even those to whom he might consider himself ostensibly hostile. Thus Propertius 1.5 begins by warning a potential rival, Gallus, to steer clear of Cynthia, but by the end of the poem, the lover is able to envisage embracing in tears of mutual comfort a Gallus who has fallen in love with Cynthia and suffers in the same way that he has. As the lover looks at his beloved, he sees her simultaneously through the eyes of *any* man who might appreciate her beauty, and with whom he would therefore have a point of identification, and he projects the jealousy that is a constitutive element of his love on to his beloved as 'behaviour' that is 'causing' that jealousy. Thus the Propertian lover accuses his beloved of taking pleasure in selling herself (*vendere*, 1.2.4) by making herself up. Similar considerations might be inferred for the Ovidian lover from the passage later in the poem (47ff.) when he suggests that the loss of her hair will hurt his beloved most when she is mistakenly admired for the wig she will have to wear.

The beloved has her own 'strategies' for negotiating her lover's attempts discursively to manoeuvre her, as we shall see. The beloved's wishes, impulses and desires will not coincide with and be a perfect match for those of the lover. The lover's discourse tries to suppress awareness of these impulses and desires, but it constantly asserts itself in his desire to control her (as in his repeated requests to her to stop dyeing her hair), to deny or restrict her autonomy, her attempts to be a person in her own right. This lover's discourse is thus working to depersonalize the beloved, to make of her a tractable object. He may rationalize this to himself and to her as an 'aesthetic preference' for 'natural' beauty, as he implicitly does in his comparisons of her hair to 'natural' objects like silk (6), spider's thread (7–8) or trees (11–12), but there is at issue here as well the struggle of the lover through his discourse to control the beloved, to mould her into the fulfilment of his desires. A lover's discourse can

---

[8] Barthes (1979), 129.

[9] See Barthes (1979), 87–92 on the lover's sense of 'disreality'.

depersonalize the beloved also by reducing the beloved to one or two, usually physical, features which are fetishized in the lover's desire – eyes, legs, breasts, maybe, or hair, as in the case of the Ovidian lover. He sees the loss of her hair not in terms of the effect upon the beloved, the immediate shock of the discovery or the more long-lasting social consequences (eventually addressed only in 45–50), but as the loss of an attribute which he identifies with his desire, as in 19–22, where he drifts off into a reminiscence of how exciting he found the object of his love in the early morning when her hair was all in disarray before she had had a chance to style it. The fetishization extends in this lover's discourse to his identification of himself with the beloved's hair, expressed in the characteristic homology: I am to you as your hair is to you. Her treatment of her hair thus becomes a surrogate in his discourse for her treatment of him, as in 13–14, where her hair is said to have been tractable (*dociles*), and never the cause of any pain to her. In 25–6, the lover recalls how patiently her hair submitted to iron and fire, referring of course to curling tongs. But the hair is personified; in this lover's discourse, it is imagined as feeling pain in order to serve the beloved's pleasure. The source of that pain is described in significantly ambiguous terms, for 'iron and fire' could also describe implements of torture, the treatment meted out to slaves, and in elegiac erotic discourse the lover presents himself as the 'slave' of his mistress (as in Propertius 1.1.27–8, discussed in chapter 3 above). The lover's discourse attempts to fix a particular application of a term, particular 'metaphors', as 'reality', and the common self-portrait of the lover as 'slave' and his beloved as his *domina*, his mistress, can be considered, from the point of view of its rhetoric, as supporting the lover's position in his manipulation of the balance of erotic power. He wants his beloved (and perhaps his readers too) to think that he is a 'real' slave, while in certain respects he could be viewed as the dominator. Referring to the beloved as *domina* ostensibly attributes all 'power' to her whilst at the same time seeking to bind her into a relationship in which the exercise of that 'power' is a function of the fulfilment of the lover's desire. In terms of erotic phenomenology, a lover may well experience being in love as a loss of mastery or control, as 'enslavement' to his beloved or to his own desire; but against the rhetorical pull of 'enslavement' as loss of freedom, the invocation of this notion could be seen as at some level a chosen strategy in an eroto-rhetorical trial of strength.[10]

[10] See Halperin (1990), 32n.

Just as it is possible to speculate whether the term *amor*/love can ever mean 'the same' to two people, and thus to see it as essentially contested[11] and the site for a struggle to fix or impose a meaning, so the language of *dolor*/pain is a focus for appropriation within lovers' discourse. Elegiac lovers make frequent reference to, and show of, the 'pain' the beloved causes, and also the lover's infinite willingness to undergo this pain. The Propertian lover invokes the mythical Milanion to construct his own situation: he succeeded with Atalanta by being prepared to undergo any hardship on behalf of the 'hard-hearted daughter of Iasius' (*durae . . . Iasidos*, 1.1.9–10). The implication of the identification is that he undergoes any and every toil for his hard-hearted Cynthia, though he expresses confusion that this 'well-tried' tactic does not seem to 'work' in his case (17–18). The language of pain involves a subtle attempt at coercion. The lover, by making such a spectacle of his suffering, and by implying that this pain is knowingly afflicted by someone hard-hearted, is trying to impose on the beloved a self-image of hard-heartedness which she may very well wish to reject as not being 'really' her. But how can she reject the imposition of this image upon her in a way that is going to 'prove' to the lover that she is not 'really' like that? There is only one way within the discourse in which she is being entrapped and her identity constructed for her: by submission (sexual or otherwise) to the lover. The lover's discourse emerges as an incessant attempt to control, to mould, to construct for the beloved an identity (as 'object') that she will accept or reject in the same way, by 'giving' herself to the lover.[12] 'Incessant', for within the lover's discourse, the achievement of 'real' love is always deferred. Whatever is 'achieved' emotionally or physically can never turn out to be the 'real' thing, and the search for 'authenticity' begins afresh. *amor* is an anagram of *mora*,[13] and on one occasion the Ovidian lover sees fit to castigate his beloved and her existing partner for colluding in her adultery with him, and thus depriving the lover of the deferral which is the space within which his discourse operates (*Amores* 2.19). Even in a society in which social structure may guarantee ready sexual availability

---

[11] See ch. 2 above.

[12] *dare* ('to give') is a very common elegiac idiom of sexual (but never *just* sexual) compliance; see Pichon (1902), s.v.

[13] Played on in e.g. Prop. 1.3.43–4, [Cynthia speaking] *deserta querebar|externo longas saepe in amore moras* ('left on my own, I complained to myself of the long periods you often spend in making love to somebody else'), Ov. *Am.* 1.6.13, *nec mora, venit amor* ('without delay, love came'); Pucci (1978) explores some related themes.

in one way or another, object 'choice' may be developed, determined and prosecuted within strategies of *unattainability*, with even the ostensibly 'attainable' being projected as 'beyond reach' within the lover's discourse.

The depersonalization of the beloved is further evinced in *Amores* 1.14 by the way that the lover becomes absorbed in his reminiscences of the beloved's hair for their own sake, irrespective of what effect this may be having on her feelings. In 9–10, his convoluted attempt to find the 'right' term to describe the colour of her hair,

> nec tamen ater erat neque erat tamen aureus ille
> sed, quamvis neuter, mixtus uterque color

Its colour was not however black, nor yet was it gold, but though neither, it was a bit of both

not only serves to ground the identity of the female in a male taxonomy of physical attractions ('not a brunette, nor yet a blonde'), but the contemplation of possible alternatives evokes the desire of the lover of *Amores* 2.4 to possess all women of all types,[14] to 'have' not an individual, but Woman. When the lover finally finds the comparison which satisfies him ('the colour of cedar when the bark is stripped off'), he is not content to leave it at that, but must expand it to satisfy his desire for expression (11–12):

> qualem clivosae madidis in vallibus Idae
> ardua derepto cortice cedrus habet

The colour the tall cedar has in the damp valleys of hilly Ida when its bark has been stripped away

A poetic cliché, perhaps, but the lover's discourse is often 'poetic' in its diction and expression, and 'naturalizes' and 'legitimizes' itself *as* poetry, a technique of self-empowerment in the rhetorical engagement with the beloved exemplified in *Amores* 1.3, where the lover seeks to attract a beloved by offering her the prospect of fame in his poetry, and asks her to 'make yourself available to me as a fertile source of subject-matter for poems' (*te mihi materiem felicem in carmina praebe*, 19). The writer of *Amores* 1.14 may be emphasizing this element in his character's discourse in 7–8 by the lover's comparison of the fineness of the beloved's hair to

---

[14] On colours of hair cf. 2.4.39–44.

spiders' thread in terms which also have currency in the description of the Callimachean poet's fine-spun poem.[15] This could connote a high estimation of personal ability, but if the *materia*, the subject-matter, of elegy is *longas compta puella comas* (*Am.* 1.1.20), a girl with combed long locks, this lover/poet has got a big problem. Further depersonalization comes in the shift between the use of second and third persons to allude to the beloved. Second person pronouns and verbs at least acknowledge her presence as another person, but when he slips into the use of the third person (17, 20, 21), it could be said that in the self-absorption of his discourse the lover loses even his vestigial awareness of that.

From the start of the poem – and the opening line suggests a dramatic situation stretching back long before it – the lover has been seeking the beloved's submission. In 45–50, he pictures for her a future in which she will have to wear a wig, and when she draws expressions of admiration, she will blush to think that her admirers are bestowing on her what properly should be given to the Sygambrian from whose hair the wig is made. It was a custom of German tribes to cut their hair and offer it to their conquerors as a sign of submission.[16] In the context of such an allusion, the posture of the beloved, her head bowed as she looks at the locks she lifts from her lap (53), must seem to the lover to figure his own triumph. The beloved has been silent throughout, but not all discourse is verbal. The lover describes how she cannot hold back her tears and covers her face with her hand as her cheeks colour with red (51–2). What do tears signify? What does 'redness' mean? Anger? Frustration? Shame? Embarrassment? All of these? Are we in any better position than the lover to interpret, to 'speak for' the beloved? In the moment of his apparent triumph, he characterizes her signals (*lacrumas male* continet *oraque dextra* | protegit, 'she cannot *confine* her tears and *protects* her face with her hand') in terms also applicable to warfare, the language of the *militia amoris*. As 'battle' is resumed, the lover changes tactics and offers 'peace' (55–6).

Reading *Amores* 1.14 as a dramatic mimesis of the lover's discourse entails the opening out of a distinction between the poet who writes the poem and the lover depicted within it, and represents the poet as a shrewd observer and critic of lovers' rhetoric. This has the consequence of recuperating Ovid from the charges of 'heartlessness' that the poet so

---

[15] Cf. esp. Virgil *Ecl.* 6.5, *deductum dicere carmen*, and Eisenhut (1961).
[16] See McKeown (1989), 382.

often attracts.[17] It can also serve to place the critic who produces such a reading as on the side of the angels. However, as well as projecting a comforting self-image of virtuousness, in suggesting the penetration through 'deception' to a 'real' understanding of the lover's discourse, it can also function as a strategy of ingratiation within the critic's discourse (*quo magis, o, faciles . . . este, puellae*). The critique must therefore be pursued further into the scholarly texts which invoke the notion of a lover's discourse.

The contemporary discourse of sexuality and gender offers the most challenging recent discussion within classical studies of love from the point of view of its being a discursive artefact, a system of conventions. It takes as its key text Longus' *Daphnis and Chloe*, reading it as an exploration of La Rochefoucauld's maxim, and as an illustration of the interplay between the terms 'nature' and 'convention'. The narrative is presented by the narrator as the description of a marvellous painting he came upon in a grove sacred to the Nymphs on the island of Lesbos which so enthralled him by the beauty of its execution and its erotic content that he was seized by a desire to emulate it in narrative form. Daphnis and Chloe grow up as foundlings 'naturally' innocent of matters to do with sex. As the feelings the pair have for each other (which the readers, but not Daphnis and Chloe, recognize as 'erotic desire') begin to emerge, the question arises of what might be attributed to 'nature' and what to 'acculturation' in the description of their education in *erōs*. Although they are innocent of conventional patterns of courtship, their behaviour is at times reminiscent of them. According to the novel, they are doing what comes naturally, so when they compare themselves to berries or plants or pelt each other with apples, what might have been taken to be the 'conventions' of pastoral romance are instead attributed to 'nature'.[18] Or similarly, when they 're-invent' the kiss via a drinking cup,[19] their action could be interpreted as 'renaturalizing' what might readily be assumed in any other case to be a 'convention'. Thus Froma Zeitlin is led to characterize *Daphnis and Chloe* as a 'naturalizing artifact': 'By this phrase', she explains,[20] 'I mean to suggest that its quality as erotic exemplar seems to tease out the varying assumptions that underlie the themes, content, and forms of romance as well as all the other erotic genres it absorbs into itself as though it were their zero degree

---

[17] See e.g. Barsby (1973), 153 on *Am*. 1.14.   [18] 1.24; see Zeitlin (1990), 439.

[19] 3.8; see Winkler (1990), 114.   [20] Zeitlin (1990), 422.

radical and could therefore attest to some organic or "natural" truth about the conduct of *erōs*.' The slippage between the two terms, the capacity for 'nature' to be 'conventionalized' or 'convention' to be 'naturalized', can be dramatic, and the closure imposed on the 'nature/culture' debate, no less than the 'answers' that this text 'offers', is a function of the ideological perspective of the reader. However much the capacity for slippage is admitted, the essentializing move that makes 'conventions' *actually* rooted in nature or those practices attributed to 'nature' *actually* conventions can only be deferred, and will be enacted sooner or later, more or less openly. For example, in appropriating the text to illustrate a discourse of female sexual vulnerability, Winkler argues that 'it is [Chloe] whose body is discovered to be "essentially" (that is, conventionally) vulnerable to sexual wounding. The lesson Chloe is taught is that "nature" itself (which I take to be a name for those *cultural* imparities that are usually regarded as unquestionable) seems to endorse the painful conventions of male-prominent, phallocentric society.'[21] Zeitlin provides a reading of *Daphnis and Chloe* which 'implies there might be some deep psychological "validity" to the recognizable generic conventions the work deploys and some underlying "natural" rationale for their construction'.[22] Her use of inverted commas signifies an attempt to represent her comments about the 'renaturalization' of the 'conventions' of *eros* as a phenomenon internal to *Daphnis and Chloe*, free from implication for Zeitlin's discourse itself. However, scholarly writing can be seen to function as no less a 'naturalizing artifact' than the texts it discusses. In a discourse in which 'convention' functions as the master term, as the point of perspective, the zero degree radical or whatever, the term can be '(re-)naturalized' by projecting what are represented as 'conventions' in the prevailing rhetoric of reality as transhistorically valid. Thus in his ostensibly historicizing discussion of this text which reads it in the (universalizing) terms of the 'pain of sexual acculturation' (symbolized in a characteristic appeal to the corporeal, in this case the image of the bruise) and the 'traumatic notion that adult female sexuality is a kind of inescapable vulnerability',[23] and inscribes it into a discourse of 'the inherent violence of the cultural system' as manifested in 'the unequal impact of that violence' on the sexes,[24] Winkler assimilates its textual phenomena to 'ordinary Mediterranean

[21] Winkler (1990), 117; the italics are Winkler's.
[22] Zeitlin (1990), 421.   [23] Winkler (1990), 104.   [24] Winkler (1990), 103.

discourse', 'Mediterranean norms generally', 'observable Mediterranean behaviour', 'the normal caution and restraint of Mediterranean social intercourse', 'the agonistic quality of Mediterranean life'.[25] Daphnis and Chloe, described by Winkler as 'natural lovers', re-invent conventional patterns of seduction;[26] but in a reprise of the rhetorical strategies attributed to the text, Chloe's innocent 'aggressive' sexual experiments as she helps to bathe Daphnis (1.13) are explained in terms of her *as some country person might put it . . .* coming into heat'.[27] You may drive 'nature' out with a pitchfork, but it will always return – as 'convention'. And *vice versa*, of course.

Any phenomenon is thus open to representation as being in accordance with 'nature' or 'convention', and can even seem to oscillate mesmerically between the two. By characterizing his narrative as the description of a picture, the narrator of *Daphnis and Chloe* situates it within a chain of representations, and we find ourselves back in the problematic of chapter 1: (where) does the chain stop? Does imitation of 'art' at some point find closure in imitation of 'life'? Zeitlin remarks that the picture's 'tangible presence, to be sure, may guarantee a certain objective authority for the narrator's tale . . . The narrator is the last in the chain of transmission from what lies behind the story as a lived reality . . . As an erotic representation, both the picture and the narrative are substitutes for the "real thing".'[28] Similarly, to describe the lover's discourse as a 'script' seems to leave it at one stage removed from 'reality'. But Zeitlin works to dissolve the distinction between 'art' and 'life' by pressing the term *mimesis* to cover all activity: 'As the narrator imitates the painting, and the narrative works its mimetic effect upon its readers, so in their way the children learn about *erōs* through a mimesis that extends throughout their entire world in their relations to nature, animals, gods, parents, elders, and themselves. The text shows an education as a prolonged and varied set of exercises in imitation that discovers the world and the self and the other by learning what can and ought to be imitated and what, we must also stress, cannot.'[29] The narrator's location of his narrative within a chain of representations serves a further function when viewed from this perspective of mimesis: 'the boldness of Longus' experiment suggests that *at a certain level of analysis*, love and letters are inseparable, that one's only means for

---

[25] The quotes come from Winkler (1990), 107, 108, 110, 111 and 117 respectively.
[26] Winkler (1990), 114.   [27] Winkler (1990), 116, italics mine.
[28] Zeitlin (1990), 434–5.   [29] Zeitlin (1990), 435.

apprehending any experience of *erōs* is already entirely shaped and determined by the cultural system of representations, including and especially stories about love.'[30] Pressing the terms 'mimesis', 'representation' and 'convention' to this degree results in the rhetoric flipping over so that it becomes 'natural' to represent. Representation thus becomes '(re-)naturalized', and the 'reality' or 'truth' of love is now situated in its discursive status.

The 'naturalization' of love as a cultural system is often effected precisely by its insertion within a chain of representations. Thus Kundera, within a novelistic exploration of love as story-shaped and fictive in *The Unbearable Lightness of Being*, 'grounds' his treatment in an appeal to Tolstoy's *Anna Karenina* (a copy of which his heroine carries under her arm in the early part of the novel), in which Anna's first meeting with Vronsky at the railway station when someone is run down by a train is symmetrically mirrored at the end of the novel when Anna commits suicide under the wheels of a train. Cautioning his readers against assuming that such notions are 'untrue to life', he asserts that human lives are composed in precisely such a fashion.[31] In *A Lover's Discourse*, which similarly 'grounds' itself in repeated allusions to Goethe's *The Sorrows of Young Werther*, Schubert's *Winterreise* and other exemplars of romantic passion,[32] Barthes invokes the notion of identification. The lover, like Werther, ceaselessly identifies himself with other lovers: 'I devour every amorous system with my gaze and in it discern the place which would be mine if I were part of that system', the Barthesian lover's voice asserts.[33] The capacity of this process to be all-consuming is remarked upon by the Ovidian lover when, after cataloguing the female attributes that attract him and the mythological figures to whom he assimilates them, he remarks that his love accommodates itself to all stories (*omnibus historiis se meus aptat amor, Am.* 2.4.44). The Propertian lover explicitly offers his poems as accounts which future unhappy lovers will be able to identify with and benefit from:

> me legat assidue post haec neglectus amator
>   et prosint illi cognita nostra mala.　　　　　　(1.7.13–14)

Let the spurned lover read me avidly after this, and may his learning of my sufferings be of advantage to him.

[30] Zeitlin (1990), 439, italics mine.　　[31] Kundera (1984), 52.
[32] The rhetorical strategies of this chapter could be analysed similarly.
[33] Barthes (1979), 129.

This chain of representations can be viewed from the opposite direction also. In Flaubert's *Madame Bovary*, Emma's enslavement to her lover Rodolphe is an enslavement to the plots of magazine fiction which she has completely internalized in her beliefs and actions, and she is driven to destruction because she would rather die than live a life that did not correspond to a romance. 'Werther identifies himself with the madman, with the footman. As a reader, I can identify myself with Werther. Historically, thousands of subjects have done so, suffering, killing themselves, dressing, perfuming themselves, writing as if they were Werther . . . A long chain of equivalences links all the lovers in the world.'[34] Thus inserted into a chain of representations, erotic experience becomes a web of intertextual allusion. So when the narrator of Ovid *Amores* I.2 cheerfully submits to love, he does so in the very word, *cedamus*, which Virgil's Gallus uses after his agonized struggle:

> omnia vincit Amor: et nos cedamus Amori.   (*Ecl.* 10.69)

> Love conquers everything: let us also yield to Love.

A reading of Roman elegy can be 'naturalized' by its being represented as a *dramatic mimesis* of the lover's discourse, thus inserting it into this infinite chain of representations. Within this chain, not only can the distinction between life and letters be dissolved, but also that between erotics and aesthetics. In the preface to *Daphnis and Chloe*, the narrator situates his narrative as a re-presentation of a painting that depicted 'everything pertaining to *erōs*', which he was stimulated to emulate as he gazed upon it. The term he uses to refer to this stimulus, *pothos*, can refer to sexual desire as well, and brings the act of aesthetic contemplation, looking at pictures or reading texts and the identificatory processes involved, within the sphere of arousal so as to create a poetics of desire or alternatively an erotics of art. If 'love' can be viewed as structured discursively, as a story with a *telos*, discourse can equally be viewed as structured in terms of 'love', with sexual climax providing a model of 'closure', immediately satisfying, but temporary and provisional in that the apprehension of 'the real thing' is always deferred, and the quest must be ever renewed. In which direction will the tenor of signification be deemed to flow? If 'erotics' can be represented in the terms of scholarship, then 'scholarship' is equally open to representation in terms of erotics. As we saw in the last chapter, Ovid structures his *Ars amatoria* in terms of the sexual act. The simultaneously sexual and rhetorical 'climax' at the

---

[34] Barthes (1979), 131.

close of Book 2, though it provides an immediately satisfying closure, is not the end of the poem, however. It is not unknown for scholarly discourse to be the vehicle for seduction, at least of its readers. Barthes conceptualizes the act of reading in terms of 'plaisir' and 'jouissance',[35] and scholarly discourse seeks mastery, to make of its 'object' a 'possession for all time', a *ktēma es aiei*.

The applicability of the term *amores* both to the object of love and to the form in which that object is represented within a discourse where the domain of 'love' is world-wide (cf. Ovid *Amores* 1.1.15, *an, quod ubique, tuum est?*), where everything is seen in terms of 'love', renders the act of making love and the act of writing about it open to being seen as manifestations of a single sphere of activity.[36] A discourse on love works to dissolve even the generic boundaries it ostensibly creates, as in the tension, or is it overlap, between elegy and bucolic in Virgil's Tenth *Eclogue*, or in the quotation from Barthes which I have included in my own preface. A discourse on love is a lover's discourse in the desire *to know*.

[35] Barthes (1975).
[36] Similarly the applicability of the verb *ludere* and the noun *lusus* to both amorous and poetic dalliance (cf. especially Cat. 50 and see Pichon 1902, s.v. 'ludere') figures the union of what are otherwise considered two separate things. *ludere* is also, of course, 'to deceive'.

An irregular in love's army: the problems of identification

What's 'in' a name? *Cynthia* in the elegies of Propertius is both a proper name and, as the first word of the first book, the title of the book as well, according to the convention of referring to books by their opening words. Just as *arma*, the first word of Virgil's *Aeneid*, serves as a title for the poem and as a generic marker (this poem has warfare as its theme and hence is an epic), so *Cynthia* serves as a generic marker in the poetry of Propertius (these poems have a woman as their theme and hence are love elegies). Thus in Propertius 1.7, the epic of Ponticus and the elegy of Propertius are differentiated and characterized respectively by the words *arma* (2, 'weapons') and *domina* (6, 'mistress'). *arma* and *Cynthia* are both signifiers, but a subtle distinction emerges in the categorization of *arma* as a common noun and *Cynthia* as a proper noun. Whilst there is ready acceptance that *arma* can signify many things – weapons, warfare, epic poetry, the male genitalia – even that these can be interlocking links in a chain of signification, there is often reluctance to accept that *Cynthia* can do other than refer to a person. A so-called 'proper' noun seems to demand a single point or object of reference in a way that a 'common' noun does not. The derivation of the grammatical term from *proprius* ('one's own') seems to guarantee that the noun is an (or the) exclusive property of the person to whom it refers.

The concept of the proper noun is also indicative of the way in which the body is so often represented as a closure on the processes of signification, taken to be undeniably a 'thing-in-itself', an embodiment, indeed, of the notion that identity is at some level immanent. The use of a proper noun, a name, especially invites the kind of reading of a text that looks through it to a reality behind it. Realism exploits this reading practice, asking its readers to see the names that appear in its texts as people. In this way, grammatical categories, rather than pre-existing reading practices, are complicit with them. The techniques of realism can be variously employed to represent the 'fictional' and the 'actual', and certain kinds of writing set out to demarcate a firm distinction between the two and place themselves on one side or the other. There are also kinds of writing which exploit realism to blur that distinction or render it problematical. In elegy, the lover-narrator uses the first-person pronoun, refers to himself on occasions as 'Propertius', 'Tibullus' or 'Ovid' and describes himself as a poet. Because neither their contemporaries nor we have any reason to doubt the existence of authors bearing those names who wrote these texts, there is an almost irresistible tendency to assimilate the author to the lover in the text, to read these poems as confessional and to regard Cynthia, Delia or Corinna as figures who existed historically outside the text of the poems. These appear to be the assumptions that have guided their reading for many, if not most, readers of these poems in both ancient and modern times, and have generated the sort of questions that have been asked about them then and now: who was Cynthia (or Delia or Corinna)? Was that her real name? What social status did she have – noblewoman, courtesan, *demi-mondaine*?

Much of what has been written in modern scholarly discourse of elegy invokes to one end or another the rather sparse discussions of this set of questions that survive from the ancient world. One text in particular, Apuleius' *Apologia*, a self-defence against the charge of using magical practices, is repeatedly cited in modern discussions. In an attempt to prejudice the case against Apuleius, his accusers apparently read out love poems in which he praised under pseudonyms a couple of slave-boys belonging to a friend, and in the following passage, he seeks to counter this attempt:

> eadem igitur opera accusent C. Catullum, quod Lesbiam pro
> Clodia nominarit, et Ticidam similiter, quod quae Metella erat
> Perillam scripserit, et Propertium, qui Cynthiam dicat, Hostiam
> dissimulet, et Tibullum, quod ei sit Plania in animo, Delia in
> versu. equidem C. Lucilium, quamquam sit iambicus, tamen
> improbarim, quod Gentium et Macedonem pueros directis
> nominibus carmine suo prostituerit. quanto modestius tandem
> Mantuanus poeta, qui itidem ut ego puerum amici sui Pollionis
> bucolico ludicro laudans et abstinens nominum sese quidem
> Corydonem, puerum vero Alexin vocat.   (10)

So, by the same token they should accuse Catullus on the grounds that he used the name Lesbia instead of Clodia, and similarly Ticidas on the grounds that he wrote Perilla for the one who was actually Metella, and Propertius, who spoke of Cynthia to conceal the identity of Hostia, and Tibullus on the grounds that he had Plania in mind but Delia in his verse. And moreover, I should criticize Lucilius, although he is a writer of satiric verse, on the grounds that he prostituted the slave-boys Gentius and Macedo in his poetry under their real names. How much more restrained is the poet of Mantua who, like me, praising the slave-boy of his friend Pollio in playful bucolic verse and refraining from using real names, calls himself Corydon and the boy Alexis.

The interpretation of this passage is then accommodated to the limits within which discussion is deemed valid or legitimate. Gordon Williams[1] dismisses the statement about Virgil's Second *Eclogue* as reflecting the allegorizing interpretation to which the *Eclogues* were subjected from a time soon after their composition, yet he accepts the statements about the elegists, saying that 'there is no reason to deny that [Apuleius] had accurate sources of information on Roman love-poetry which may well have been more or less contemporary with the composition of the poetry.'[2] Why should these sources, if indeed they did exist, be any more accurate or informed than the 'allegorizing interpretations' of the *Eclogues* which were so summarily dismissed? Within the rhetoric of this 'historicizing' discourse, 'allegorizing' and 'interpretation' are both pejorative terms in that they suggest the appropriation of the text, the originary meaning of which is located in this interpretative scheme in the 'time of composition'. In chapter I above, I suggested that any act of interpretation negotiates a tension between a hermeneutics which seeks out an originary meaning for a text and the appropriation of the text by, and its accommodation to, the matrix of practices and beliefs out of which the interpretation is produced. In the process of interpretation, the text thus has a role, which may be obvious or occluded depending on the way in which this tension is negotiated, in the authorization of the beliefs, practices and institutions which inform the interpretation. In much recent scholarly writing on elegy, an unproblematized historicism, with its rhetoric of objectivity effacing its own historicity, operates to identify interpretation with hermeneutics, and to mask appropriation, either

---

[1] Williams (1968), 526–7.   [2] Williams (1968), 528.

relegating it to a secondary sphere of 'reception' or projecting it as a disreputable other. This historicizing, hermeneutical approach, in seeing history as in some way *already determined*, must marginalize the notion of appropriation insofar as that notion suggests that history is an open-ended process, continuing here and now. This is not to advocate that we simply reverse the hierarchy and privilege appropriation at the expense of hermeneutics (for that is to efface the historicity of an appropriative interpretation), but to recognize that each term is not separate from the other, but involves it. Heidegger makes the point thus: 'We question historically if we ask what is still happening even if it seems to be past.'[3] If a discourse calling itself 'hermeneutics' represents Roman elegy as a thing already historically determined and awaiting the 'discovery' of the determinants immanent in it, a discourse calling itself 'appropriation' represents interpretations of elegy similarly. All interpretation seeks to make of its 'texts' *objects*, circumscribed and historically situated, whether those 'texts' be Propertius' elegies, Apuleius' comments upon them, Williams' *Tradition and Originality in Roman Poetry*, or, indeed, men and women.

The argument, again 'grounded' in an ancient text (the scholiast's note on Horace, *Odes* 2.12) and so discursively legitimized, that the 'fictitious' names correspond in their number of syllables with the 'real' names, and that further, as Richard Bentley (a significant focus of authority within this discourse) asserted, they are exact metrical substitutes for the 'real' names, is described by Williams as 'impressive'[4] even as it is conceded that Hostia, beginning as it does with a vowel, cannot always be substituted for Cynthia. The information about the identities of the women in elegy is deemed to be confirmed also by the identification of Lesbia as Clodia; indeed, it is asserted that 'an inappropriate degree of scepticism is needed to question' this identification. Once again, 'inappropriate' is used without further definition in an effort to determine what it is and is not legitimate to entertain as an idea in a particular scholarly discourse; the 'reality' of the objection is dismissed along with its 'propriety'.[5] Marriage between the lover and his beloved seems to be impossible (e.g. Propertius 2.7), so the beloved is assumed either to be an

---

[3] Quoted in Attridge, Bennington and Young (1987), 8.   [4] Williams (1968), 527.
[5] Williams (1968), 528. Williams of course mentions Catullus 79, which offers an invitation to uncover the 'real' identity of Lesbia; but the notion of propriety is invoked here, as we shall see, to render unproblematic what may be involved in the idea of 'identification'.

aristocratic woman involved in an affair which needed for social reasons to be kept to a greater or lesser degree clandestine (and thus the names Cynthia or Delia are pseudonyms – so Williams, assuming that Lesbia can be identified unproblematically with Clodia, and then taking this as his model for the elegiac relationship); or else more commonly a *meretrix*, a freedwoman with whom an aristocrat might carry on an affair but whom, in the face of the social norms engendered by an aristocratic ideology, it would not so much as cross his mind to marry. The assumption that the poems are in some way a record of, and inspired by, love for a specific historical woman underlies a common reading procedure, namely that any poem addressed to an unnamed girl must be addressed to the named beloved, and this goes both for earlier critics who try to reconstruct a historical sequence for the affair[6] and for more recent ones[7] who reject the possibility of reconstructing a narrative of the affair whilst nonetheless accepting its historicity. Such, remarks Paul Veyne,[8] is the power of the running title. Because the opening word of the first book of Propertius suggests a title *Cynthia*, the assumption is that every woman addressed but not named is Cynthia. However true this may be for Book 1, Veyne observes that Cynthia is named only three times in Book 3. One poem in that book (3.20) has often been held to contain biographical information about the 'real' Cynthia, namely that the addressee is said to have a 'learned ancestor' (8), for which the commentators have unearthed the name of an otherwise obscure epic poet Hostius on the assumption that Cynthia is being addressed in this poem and that Cynthia is 'really' someone called Hostia. Veyne however suggests that this poem can be read as a declaration of love to an unnamed but marriageable girl.

To invoke another distinction discussed in my opening chapter, the more 'historicizing' an account, the more it tends to occlude the textuality of that which it posits as its object, and *vice versa*. An analysis such as Williams', which I have here represented as instantiating the unacknowledged assumptions and patterns of authority of the scholarly discourse of which it is part, occludes not only the textuality of the poems it is discussing, but also the textuality of the ancient sources that are adduced as ostensibly independent evidence. Apuleius' *Apology* or the scholiast's comments on Horace's *Odes* are not privileged pass keys to

---

[6] See e.g. Butler and Barber (1933), xxi.
[7] See e.g. Lyne (1980), 62–3. [8] Veyne (1988), 57.

the truth of elegy or the historical existence of the women depicted there. A 'textualizing' approach will adduce these passages as evidence of *one* way in which elegy could be read at the time, as the covert record of an affair. Such an approach would emphasize the way in which elegy emerged within a discursive situation in which its texts will have been shaped by the expectation of the response, the reading practices, they would meet with and will have accommodated themselves to or otherwise interacted with that response. From this perspective, the case of Gallus becomes particularly intriguing. Contemporary texts make reference to a freedwoman named Volumnia who, it was said, had relationships with Mark Antony and Gallus. She is represented as a figure of notoriety; her lifestyle and profession, mime actress, ensured that her name carried with it connotations of scandal. Volumnia's stage-name, Cytheris, merits some comment, as it is not *just* a name (no name is just the simple designation of a particular individual), but serves to represent an *identity*. Freedwomen who made a living with their bodies often adopted Greek names (Chloe, Glycera, Phyllis, etc.) which effectively signified their sexual availability if the price was right. The name Cytheris is similarly 'Greek', but has further connotations. It is formed from the name of a place, the island of Cythera, the most famous association of which was that it was sacred to Venus. So the name Cytheris could connote something about the actress or the roles she played. Gallus writes elegies addressed to a woman named Lycoris, again a 'Greek' name, again a name formed from a place name, in this case a place on Mt Parnassus, Lycoreia, sacred to Apollo, and the origin of one of the god's cult titles, Apollo Lycoreus, which seems to be particularly associated with his role as god of poetry.[9] Thus the name Lycoris could say something about both the beloved's socio-sexual status and the role she played in Gallus' poetry, and in the Qaṣr Ibrîm fragment she appears as representing the standard of excellence to which the poet's elegies aspire:

> . . . tandem fecerunt carmina Musae
> quae possem domina deicere digna mea.   (fr. 4.1–2 Buechner)

. . . at last the Muses fashioned poems which I might declare worthy of my mistress.

If such was the discursive situation in which the poems of Gallus appeared, a context in which it was known or assumed that Gallus ('the

---

[9] See Anderson, Parsons and Nisbet (1979), 148n.115.

poet') had a liaison with the actress Cytheris, the reader's sense of eavesdropping and being in the know (however illusory this may have been) would be part of the attraction of reading elegy, a predisposition open to exploitation by the elegist, and not only in what he wrote: the behaviour of Gallus will have helped to constitute the discursive context in which his poems appeared. Readers of these poems might well have seen a continuity between Lycoris and Cytheris. How was such a continuity to be explained or accounted for by readers who were convinced that it was 'there'? A reading practice, to which Catullus' 'identification' of Lesbia in poem 79 had already appealed and which it had thereby helped to reproduce, would prompt the assumption that Lycoris was a pseudonym for Cytheris and an interpretation of the poems as a covert form of autobiography; the metrical and other similarities of the names might seem to confirm such an assumption. The elegies of Gallus then in turn become part of the discursive situation in which the subsequent elegists write, name their beloveds[10] and interact with their anticipated modes of reception.

From the textualist perspective, the passage of Apuleius, suggesting a readiness to read not only the elegists but also Virgil's *Eclogues* as autobiographical, serves as testimony to a widespread ancient reading practice which treated poetry as confessional. Similarly, poem 16 of Catullus, where the poet threatens to penetrate Furius and Aurelius sexually at both ends if they persist in extrapolating an identity for him from the lewd verses he writes, can be read as making fun of this way of reading texts, this 'mode' of readerly 'reception'.[11] Seen thus, modern 'historicizing' scholarship emerges as a reprise of an ancient reading practice, and this can be represented by projecting this reading practice as either a constant or as being discursively reproduced through the manipulation by the texts of elegy of their own reception. Ovid teases his readership about Corinna on a number of occasions. In *Amores* 2.17.29–30,

> novi aliquam, quae se circumferat esse Corinnam;
> ut fiat, quid non illa dedisse velit?

he says that he knows of a woman who goes around saying that she is Corinna; what wouldn't she be willing to *give*, he remarks with the

---

[10] See Randall (1979) for a detailed investigation of the connotations of these names.
[11] See ch. 3 above.

broadest of sexual innuendoes,[12] to become her. He does not say whether there is or is not a 'real' Corinna; the joke depends on the prevarication. In *Ars* 3.538,

> et multi, quae sit nostra Corinna, rogant

he recalls, *à propos* the beloveds in the works of the other elegists, that many people ask him who his Corinna is. Significantly, he just leaves the question hanging; to offer any kind of 'answer' would be to disrupt the reading practice to which the *Amores* are accommodated. On a number of occasions, both within the *Amores*[13] and in the exile poems,[14] he flirts with admitting it was all fiction, but a categorical statement to that effect is not necessarily to be extracted from what he says. The prevarication continues, conditioning yet further the reception of his work, manipulating the discourse of which it is part, involving itself in its own reception so as to reproduce the reading practice on which the initial impact of the text depended, and to continue thereby to determine the ways in which the text is read. The 'textualizing' perspective which generates this approach of course has its 'historicizing' aspect. The question of the identity of the beloved in elegy thus becomes a history of the way the text of elegy has managed to perpetuate the reading practices to which its composition was accommodated. Apuleius becomes one chapter or episode of that history, modern scholarly discussions about the identity of the beloved another.

Viewed thus, the 'reading practice' associated with the 'historicizing' approach assumes an unproblematic equivalence between the names of beloveds and 'real' people, as Williams sees an unquestionable continuity between Lesbia and Clodia. However, to appropriate Maria Wyke's terminology and perspectives and extend them to the text of Catullus,

---

[12] On the erotic connotations of *dare* see ch. 4 above. Does *ut* (30) introduce a final or consecutive clause here? No amount of searching in the grammars will give a definitive answer.

[13] *Am* 3.12, esp. 41–4: *exit in immensum fecunda licentia vatum|obligat historica nec sua verba fide;|et mea debuerat falso laudata videri|femina; credulitas nunc mihi vestra nocet* ('the creative licence of poets knows no bounds nor binds its words by historical truth; my woman also ought to have been seen as praised under false pretences; now your credulity is doing me harm').

[14] *Tr.* 2.339–40: *ad leve rursus opus, iuvenalia carmina, veni,|et falso movi pectus amore meum* ('I turned back to a light work, the poems of my youth, and I stirred my breast with a love that was not true'); 4.10.59–60: *moverat ingenium totam cantata per urbem|nomine non vero dicta Corinna mihi* ('Corinna, celebrated in song throughout the whole city, had inspired my talent, sung of by me under a name that wasn't real').

Lesbia no less than Cynthia is a 'written woman', a *scripta puella*,[15] a manifestation of modes of representation of the female, and cannot be identified with, or separated from, a historical figure in any straightforward way. A further twist can be administered to this textualist turn, and it can be asserted that Clodia, Volumnia and indeed any other historical figures are themselves also 'written women' or 'written men' in the sense that their identities are discursively constituted. At what point does one impose closure on this mode of analysis? 'Maria Wyke' too can be viewed as a 'written woman', the 'embodiment' of the discourses of which she is the focus. Indeed, she becomes 'identified' by and with the 'themes' she writes about. Classical scholarship is familiar with this as the topos in which the poet is described as doing what he describes as being done, and is thus 'identified' with the themes of his work.[16]

Setting up parameters such as these allows readings of elegy to be 'placed' within them and appropriated in turn, and enables me to move on to the most ambitious of recent interpretations of elegy. Paul Veyne rejects what I have termed the 'historicizing' reading practice and the assumptions it encodes. His reading, which in the terms which I have set out makes characteristically 'textualist' moves, works to split the identity of the poet/lover: the 'I' who is the narrator of these poems is not to be identified in an unproblematic way with the poet, and the beloved is not to be considered as a person with a historical reality outside the text, but as a *theme* within it; Cynthia and Delia are types rather than specific personalities. The expression of his approach serves not only as a critique of the specific arguments of previous writers on elegy but as an ostentatious act of self-positioning within a broader intellectual formation. Thus he opens the fifth chapter of his book on elegy with a sweeping and provocative declaration: 'It is historically impossible and aesthetically absurd to identify the paramours of the Roman elegists. It would even be a hindrance to understanding their work if we were to do so, for they sing not about some particular amorous relationship but of the amorous life itself.'[17] As I suggested in chapter 1 above, arguments are developed and positions articulated in the making and manipulation of distinctions, and meaning is generated to the extent to which, in what ways, and to what ends, terms are kept distinct. Veyne's approach to elegy, in opening out a distinction between 'sociology' and 'semiotics', provides a clear illustration. To develop the point that he has just made, Veyne divides his analysis into two chapters. Chapter 5, entitled 'Not

---

[15] See Wyke (1987a).   [16] See Goodyear (1965), 119.   [17] Veyne (1988), 67.

Such High Society', presents a sociological analysis of Roman society in the period when elegy was being written, investigating the ways in which sexual attitudes and behaviour were bound up with class ideologies. Chapter 6, entitled 'From Sociology to Semiotics', examines elegy not as a representation of that society, as it is often taken to be, but as a sort of game, a form of entertainment, in which author and reader collude in playing by a fixed set of rules. Veyne lays great emphasis on this notion of elegy as game. Earlier in the book he has stated very categorically what he sees to be the basis of his view:

> The poet pretends to be a slave to some passion, to dream in vain of rustic purity, but he does not really enter into conflict with things as they are. He does not hold the world to be in error, and he does not appeal to his readers to modify their ideas regarding religious superstitions or women who are too quickly called 'loose'. Roman erotic elegy only appeals to reality in order to contrast itself to it . . . Elegy appeals to things as they are for an effect, it does not seek to change them, and this is why we shall speak of the semiotics instead of the sociology or ideology of elegy.[18]

The distinction thus generated, within this rhetoric of 'reality', between 'sociology' and 'semiotics', is insisted upon and needs explanation, with the proviso that any 'account' of Veyne's argument is of course a recontextualization in the service of this argument and not impartial.

First, chapter 5, the sociology. In presenting his picture of Roman society, Veyne deals in terms of 'ideology' rather than 'fact'. For a male aristocratic Roman, the sexual accessibility of a woman was a function of the way he perceived her as categorized socially. This ideology of class-and-sexual behaviour expressed itself in a series of stereotypes: an aristocratic lady had strict morals and could not be touched by any but her husband; a free-born plebeian woman might deceive her husband with a generous aristocrat; a freedwoman, a *libertina*, was by nature sexually promiscuous.[19] These stereotypes will to a degree have determined actual behaviour. Stereotypes are never an exact fit for the circumstances they purport to describe, and there were undoubtedly exceptions who transgressed them – rich, well-born divorcées, Veyne suggests, or widows or orphaned girls with dowries may have been able to enjoy a greater

---

[18] Veyne (1988), 29–30.   [19] Veyne (1988), 72–3.

freedom of sexual behaviour than their class position might have suggested. But stereotypes have a way of confirming themselves in the eyes of those who rely upon them. Ideologically, a group within society is regarded as inferior and despised; what the members of that group do confirms the contempt in which they are held – nothing more can be expected of them, since they 'are' like that. Ideological stereotypes *essentialize* people: that's the way they are, the way they want to be, and they are not worthy of anything else. With stereotypes exceptions don't count, and can be dismissed.[20] Freedwomen are naturally promiscuous, the stereotype goes, you can see it in the way they act. But for a female former slave, her body may be her only economic asset, and it remains an asset only so long as it remains sexually desirable. Within the freed-woman class, modes of behaviour will have developed so as to maximize the return on this diminishing asset, modes of behaviour so internalized by the women involved as to emerge as spontaneous expressions. A suitor might be inclined to give a bigger present if he thought he had a rival for her affections or if she acted indifferent; he in turn might regard this as flirting or hard-heartedness, the 'characteristic', as he would see it, behaviour of a freedwoman. The circle closes, the stereotype is confirmed. Social stereotypes single out victims and then make them responsible for the victimization inflicted upon them. For a freedwoman in Rome, economic necessity will have been inscribed in patterns of behaviour, deportment and attitude. The stereotype not only fails to acknowledge, but actually suppresses the social and economic factors determining this behaviour, instead characterizing the freedwoman as 'fickle', 'flirtatious', 'promiscuous' and 'grasping'.

Veyne's semiotic analysis of elegy in chapter 6 sees it as a system, a 'game',[21] with a defined set of rules, and what gets written about and what doesn't observes these rules, 'the internal necessities of a certain form of creation', as he puts it.[22] Given that the subject of elegy is passion and the suffering it creates, the options for a Roman author were limited, Veyne suggests. Adoring a married woman in vain was out; the Romans would have laughed at the poetry of the troubadours, he asserts.[23] The only way for a Roman to suffer poetically was to love a woman unworthy of marriage. Thus in Veyne's semiological analysis, the 'mistress' is a defining theme. As Veyne points out on the basis of a number of readings from Propertius and Tibullus,[24] the status of the beloved is not made

[20] Veyne (1988), 77.   [21] Veyne (1988), 94.   [22] Veyne (1988), 85.
[23] Veyne (1988), 86.   [24] Veyne (1988), 89–90.

explicit or consistent; her status can be vague or fluid because this is not autobiographical confession, and the only necessary condition from the poetic point of view is that she be represented as unattainable. She is, in Veyne's term, to be conceived of as an 'irregular'. In what particular way she is to be conceived of as an 'irregular' is of such secondary importance that, if it varies from poem to poem, that is neither here nor there. The lover within the poems, the narrator ('Ego', as Veyne calls him, thus emphasizing rhetorically the disjunction from the 'poet') is again a theme. Every genre, he asserts, constructs an implied reader required by the law of the genre.[25] Actual readers become that implied reader when they submit to the laws of the particular genre they are reading, for example by seeing the lover and his mistress as themes rather than identifying them with specific historical persons. Thus elegy is a form of entertainment. The ideal reader, he says, was not invited to see things from the lover's point of view, to identify with him, but to regard his enslavement and complaints as laughable.[26] This is what Veyne describes as the 'pact'[27] between the elegiac poet and the implied reader: they smile at each other as they view the behaviour of the lover. The elegiac poets may smile about what they depict, but are absolutely serious about the rules of the game.[28] Elegy is thus no less artificial and rule-bound a literary genre than Virgil's *Eclogues*, the only difference being that the characters in elegy wear city clothes and live in Rome whereas the characters in the *Eclogues* wear rustic clothes and live in the country, a theme Veyne then goes on to develop in his chapter 7.

Veyne's division of his analysis into the sociological and the semiological can be understood and justified in terms of his setting out to counter the overwhelming tendency in scholarly discourse to read these poems as confessional, as presenting a picture of their society, and, however elusive his expression, his account is nonetheless amenable to appropriation in various ways. For example, his analysis of Roman sexual behaviour in terms of ideological stereotypes which both encode and regulate class attitudes and distinctions could be 'extended' to suggest the way that recent scholarship's search for what it would wish to term 'facts' about women in elegy draws on ideologies of sexual and class behaviour that permeate and regulate contemporary society. Was Cynthia a courtesan or promiscuous noblewoman? The question is posed as one of fact

[25] Veyne (1988), 97.   [26] Veyne (1988), 86.
[27] Veyne (1988), 99.   [28] Veyne (1988), 99.

demanding a factual answer. But, as Veyne suggests, the enabling condition of elegy is that it is a lover's discourse of unattainability and so marriage with Cynthia is presented as impossible; she is an 'irregular'. Her status is undefined because there is no need to define it. A Roman reader reading any poem would accommodate it to whatever ideological stereotype of female sexual 'irregularity' or 'unattainability' seemed to be appropriate in any particular case. To arrive at its 'factual' answer (and it is to be recalled that both noblewoman and courtesan have been offered in the case of Cynthia), scholarship can be represented as going through the 'same' procedure. Cynthia is described in terms such as 'fickle', 'wanton', 'temperamental', 'grasping' and so on (terms which are prompted by the perspective of the Propertian lover's discourse), and these 'qualities' are assumed to belong *essentially* to a woman of a particular type and particular social status. An ideological stereotype of female behaviour is being invoked, and the answer is presented as a 'fact': Cynthia *is* a courtesan or Cynthia *is* a promiscuous noblewoman. Viewed in this way, this is ideology in action here and now, with scholarship's association with authority and truth making it a vehicle and source of legitimation of the ideologies that inform society. The complex process whereby social categorizations are arrived at and represented as 'natural' to the extent that they are held to constitute a person's *identity* (as in the statement that 'Cynthia *is* a courtesan') remains buried and unexamined, scholarship's 'historicizing' rhetoric concealing from its practitioners the way elegy is appropriated within its interpretations as one of the sources of legitimation of those ideologies. Griffin's references to 'drabs', 'sea-side vamps', etc.[29] from this perspective are 'really' a parade of sexual ortho*doxies*.

Having offered a 'sympathetic' reading of Veyne, I will now give a so-called 'critical' one which no less renders his text open to recontextualization and appropriation. Veyne's 'insights' are articulated within a distinction between sociology and semiotics so categorical that he denies that a mixture of the two, a sociology *of* literature, is a meaningful concept.[30] So rigid a demarcation invites further scrutiny. Veyne emphatically states that elegy leaves things as it found them: 'elegy appeals to things as they are for an effect, it does not seek to change them, and this is why we shall speak of the semiotics instead of the sociology or ideology of elegy.'[31] A couple of pages earlier, Veyne has prepared for

---

[29] See e.g. Griffin (1985), 26, 93.   [30] Veyne (1988), 91.   [31] Veyne (1988), 30.

this by the use of a phrase on which I will lay considerable emphasis: 'In order that dull people will run out of breath trying to catch up with them, the elegists create *a pure art* that is full of traps of the sort that make one believe it is not pure art, that it is sensual, sentimental, passionate.'[32] In the phrase 'a *pure* art', Veyne is constructing an aesthetic sphere free from political or social considerations, and suggesting that art ultimately is not determined by and ultimately does not have any effect upon the conditions in which it is produced. Thus 'the contingency of what might have been autobiographical events is replaced by the internal necessities of a certain form of creation';[33] '[t]he conformist type of ending *returns to zero* a narration engendered by some initial deviation. This is one reason, and the most succinct one, for not believing in the sociology of literature.'[34] The most obvious manifestation of this is Veyne's character-ization of elegy as a form of entertainment (and so its effects are not to be described as 'real'),[35] in particular his description of elegy as a game in which author and readers agree on the rules, and, by implication, agree on the interpretation. However, seeing elegy as a semiotic *system* pure and simple, as a 'game', foreswears any investigation of why it might have been viewed either as 'entertaining' or as 'shocking', why it might have 'mattered'. That is, it seeks to abstract elegy from the discursive situation in which it was produced and the assumptions which it exploited, the discursive situation by which it was shaped and in which it has been received. Thus Veyne's approach offers no reason why a reader like Apuleius regarded it as plausible to assume that when Cynthia or Delia was mentioned he should think of Hostia or Plania other than that he must not have known the rules of the game.

It is always open to us to turn the tables on Veyne and relate his defence of 'pure art', the autonomy of the aesthetic sphere, to the discursive situation in which his book was written. Veyne's position sharply differentiates him from that of Pierre Bourdieu, whose book *Distinction*[36] seeks to collapse the 'aesthetic' into the 'sociological', arguing that the discourse of artistic taste, of the ostensibly aesthetic, is a form of cultural capital which serves to enact distinctions within and between social groups. This is diametrically opposed to Veyne's idea of art as a system characterized only by the internal necessities of its creation, a *game*. Bourdieu, of course, is interested in terms like this from the point of view

---

[32] Veyne (1988), 28; italics mine.　　[33] Veyne (1988), 85.

[34] Veyne (1988) 91; italics mine.　　[35] Cf. Veyne (1988), 29–30, cited above.

[36] Bourdieu (1984).

of the politics of their invocation.[37] There is only one explicit reference to Bourdieu in Veyne's book: 'Bourdieu, whose rage at the arbitrariness of things and whose spirit of seriousness we share and understand, rightly contends that speech is not a means of communication but an instrument of action'.[38] This expression of sympathy seems to be a damaging admission. The following sentences, however, reveal not an engagement with Bourdieu so much as a lack of engagement between competing paradigms: 'as for *literary* speech, it acts in and through its implied reader and not through those social beings who are its readers. It concludes a certain pact with its implied reader, and what can and cannot be said emerges from that pact.'[39] Veyne's scheme requires a sociological sphere to correspond to his aesthetic sphere to which the 'social' or the 'political' can be relegated, safely clear of the 'aesthetic', and to that extent he is sympathetic to the sociologist Bourdieu. But whereas Bourdieu's project is to dissolve the boundary, Veyne's is to maintain it. Thus once 'speech' becomes 'literary', readership must move from the 'actual' to the 'implied'. This intellectual and methodological distinction could, following the lead of Bourdieu, be inscribed in a discourse of Parisian academic politics,[40] but though I shall be returning to consider the difference of approaches of which Veyne and Bourdieu can be used as representatives, I want first to consider the autonomy of the aesthetic in Veyne from another angle.

In representing the past, 'similarity' or 'difference' can be emphasized, thus tending to make the past fundamentally 'the same' as the present or fundamentally 'different'. In mediating its treatment through terms like 'love' which are assumed without further discussion to be historically transcendent, much recent scholarship on elegy represents the past as fundamentally 'the same' as the present. So widespread is this approach that Veyne's subtitle, *Love, Poetry and the West*, might easily be taken to promise a work with a similar approach, arguing for cultural continuities. However, although Veyne frequently invokes post-classical Western love poetry, he does so in order to emphasize its difference, its otherness, from Roman elegy. This is part of a broader strategy to present 'the West' as *punctuated* by a series of episodes, the similarities between which are illusory: 'all too often we think we recognize our own commonplaces, the eternal evidence of common sense, in ancient ideas

[37] On 'game' see Bourdieu (1990), 64–6.   [38] Veyne (1988), 175.
[39] Veyne (1988), 175; italics mine.   [40] See Bourdieu (1988).

that were implicitly very different.'[41] So, for example, love is described as a 'cultural creation',[42] specific to its various contexts. Again, the Roman world presents us with 'another conception of the individual'.[43] Roman elegy too had its own system, its own aesthetics, and it is presented as *alien*: Veyne's epilogue is entitled 'Why Ancient Poetry Bores Us'. Veyne thus also challenges the historical transcendence of the concept of the aesthetic: 'there are more different aesthetics in the past and in the future than our spontaneous dogmatism likes to admit, and we should resign ourselves to the idea that many forms of beauty are temporarily dead to our eyes'.[44] Ancient poetry bores us because our contemporary aesthetics is what Veyne calls an 'aesthetics of intensity' which 'believes it can reveal to us the final essence of things'.[45] Thus, although Veyne projects the *autonomy* of aesthetics, he does not argue, ostensibly, for its *transcendence*: 'there is no essence of art, just an infinity of styles. Every aesthetic has merit, and excludes and misjudges all others.'[46] A particular aesthetic, not least our own, is transitory and liable to sudden change. Veyne projects his concept of the aesthetic as rendering the efforts of a Bourdieu wasted: 'while sociologists continue to enquire into the distribution of tastes as a function of social class, the ground beneath our feet will change of its own accord.'[47] However, as I have argued, 'difference' can be asserted only if 'similarity' is also asserted at some level, however occluded, and *vice versa*. Although Veyne ostensibly argues against the transcendence of the aesthetic, his presentation of Roman elegy as alien is effected through the projection of it *as* an 'aesthetic'. Its characterization as a *different* aesthetic is effected by the projection upon it of a (transcendent) category, 'the aesthetic'.

The intellectual nexus between Veyne and Foucault is acknowledged by both in their writings, and Veyne's treatment of the concepts of love, the individual, aesthetics, like his treatment of economics in *Le Pain et le cirque*,[48] has the stamp of the Foucauldian *episteme*, and is subject to the same objections. However full an explication can be offered of everything within the *episteme*, nothing more interesting can be said about the shift from one to another than 'it happened'; compare what Veyne said of different aesthetics: 'the ground beneath our feet will change *of its own accord*.' The methodology leads to a crisis of historical explanation of which Veyne is acutely aware as he turns to consider the concept of truth:

---

[41] Veyne (1988), 162.   [42] Veyne (1988), 152.   [43] Veyne (1988), 65.
[44] Veyne (1988), 33.   [45] Veyne (1988), 185.   [46] Veyne (1988), 184.
[47] Veyne (1988), 186.   [48] Veyne (1976).

Human beings depend on their belief in truth, the true, the one, yet unawares we practise different, incompatible, but apparently analogous principles of truth. All these different measures of truth, however different, are only one in our eyes. The truths of other times seem analogous to our own, which allows for historical 'understanding'. This plural and analogical nature of truth also grounds aesthetics.[49]

In pursuit of what he can represent as 'the truth, the true, the one', Veyne feels obliged to jettison historical explanation as such: 'historians of literature, and historians per se, including sociologists, do not explain events, whatever they may believe. They explicate them, interpret them. Historicity is invention.'[50] Although Veyne here bundles sociologists in with historians, his own projection of sociology as a counterweight to semiotics suggests the historian's retreat under the pressure of textualist challenge into sociology as the discourse representing the 'real'. If Bourdieu collapses the aesthetic into the sociological, we are approaching the point at which Veyne will collapse the historical into the aesthetic, and abandon contingency for a metaphysical master term. 'Is there an invariant, some transhistorical essence?' he asks.[51] 'I fear this alleged essence comes down to one simple thing, open to any contingency: aestheticization ... It consists in sovereignly inventing an interpretation – and in conventional or useful cases, this interpretation gets passed off as true'. In Veyne's account, 'the truth, the true' is equated with 'the one'; as a climax to his argument, he invokes Nietzsche: aestheticization gives things 'the unity *they do not have*'.[52]

Unity implies structure, and the notion of structure raises the problematic issue of determination, the imposition of limits. This involves a bind, as Veyne can illustrate. The determination which Veyne seeks to identify, describe or impose is encoded in an ostensibly historical discourse. In the identification, description or imposition of structure, historical discourse requires the operation of closure,[53] but this ultimately entails the shutting down or disavowal of historicity through the admission of terms granted transhistorical validity. Within their limits, Veyne's *epistemes* rigorously historicize their constituent terms (love, individuality, aesthetics and so on) and deny them a transhistorical

[49] Veyne (1988), 14.   [50] Veyne (1988), 175.   [51] Veyne (1988), 175.

[52] Veyne (1988), 179; the emphasis is Veyne's.

[53] See Attridge, Bennington and Young (1987), 8–9.

validity. But the *epistemes* themselves must negotiate, or find the means to evade, the question of their own historicity. Veyne's resistance is a heroic one, but when the capitulation comes in the term 'aestheticization', it involves the invocation of, or flip into, an ostensibly distinct, indeed 'opposed', discourse[54] with ostensibly distinct modes of determination, and Veyne is by no means alone in seeking to escape the bind of history through the poeticization of history. Although history and aesthetics have long been presented as separate, even antipathetic, we are now familiar with modes of argumentation which suggest the complicity of terms that are presented as distinct, and Rodolphe Gasché has done so very effectively in the case of history and aesthetics.[55]

The *telos* of historical discourse is the imposition of closure, paradoxically the shutting down of historicity, the end of history, the last word. But whatever presents itself as 'closed' can be recontextualized as still 'open' and *vice versa*. Veyne's attempted imposition of an aesthetic determination is always open to the contention that his master term, aestheticization, projected as transhistorical, as 'outside' historical determination, is itself historically determined, that if history consists of 'fictions of factual representation',[56] those fictions are nonetheless themselves the product of historical processes. And so the debate continues. I have presented elegy as not already historically determined and circumscribed in the past and awaiting the discovery of its determination, but as a discourse in which we remain involved, a discourse constituted by all the forces that moulded the text plus its reception, including our own, in recognition of both its 'determinateness' and its 'contingency'. I have attempted to appropriate Veyne by characterizing a term of his as a hidden closure, making his book into an episode, by the imposition of a closure, in the (my) history of the reception of elegy, and my discourse lies open to recuperation in turn. The description of elegy as a 'discourse', ostensibly 'open', is achieved only by the imposition of closure, the objectification involved in any description – whatever rhetorical attempts are made to occlude it, as in the assertion that a discourse is 'open-*ended*'.

[54] As argued in ch. 1 above, terms presented ostensibly as separate and opposed when pressed appeal at some level to each other.   [55] Gasché (1987).
[56] This is the title of one of the essays in White (1978).

Bibliography

Adams, J.N. (1982) *The Latin Sexual Vocabulary*. London

Anderson, R.D., Parsons, P.J. and Nisbet, R.G.M. (1979) 'Elegiacs by Gallus from Qaṣr Ibrîm', *JRS* 69. 125–155

Attridge, D., Bennington, G and Young, R. (eds) (1987) *Post-structuralism and the Question of History*. Cambridge

Ball, T. (1988) *Transforming Political Discourse*. Oxford

Barsby, J.A. (1973) *Ovid's Amores Book One*. Oxford

Barthes, R. (1974) *S/Z*, trans. R. Miller. London

    (1975) *The Pleasure of the Text*, trans. R. Miller. London

    (1979) *A Lover's Discourse: Fragments*, trans. R. Howard. London

Boswell, J. (1980) *Christianity, Social Tolerance and Homosexuality: Gay People in Western Europe from the Beginning of the Christian Era to the Fourteenth Century*. Chicago

    (1982/3) 'Revolutions, universals and sexual categories', *Salmagundi* 58. 89–113

Bourdieu, P. (1982) *Ce que parler veut dire: l'économie des échanges linguistiques*. Paris

    (1984) *Distinction. A Social Critique of the Judgement of Taste*, trans. R. Nice. London

    (1988) *Homo Academicus*, trans. P. Collier. Cambridge

    (1990) *In Other Words. Essays towards a Reflexive Sociology*, trans. M. Adamson. Cambridge

Brink, C.O. (1971) *Horace on Poetry: the 'Ars Poetica'*. Cambridge

Butler, H.E. and Barber, E.A. (1933) *The Elegies of Propertius*. Oxford

Cairns, F. (1979) *Tibullus: a Hellenistic Poet at Rome*. Cambridge

Culler, J. (1983) *On Deconstruction*. London

Davidson, A.I. (1987/8) 'Sex and the emergence of sexuality', *Critical Inquiry* 14. 16–48

Davis, J.T. (1989) *Fictus Adulter: Poet as Actor in the Amores*. Amsterdam

Derrida, J. (1982) *Margins of Philosophy*, trans. A. Bass. Brighton

Eisenhut, W. (1961) 'Deducere carmen. Ein Beitrag zum Problem der literarischen Beziehungen zwischen Horaz und Properz', in *Gedenkschrift für Georg Rohde*. Tübingen

Felperin, H. (1990) *The Uses of the Canon*. Oxford

Foucault, M. (1972) *The Archaeology of Knowledge*, trans A.M. Sheridan Smith. London

    (1986a) 'Preface to *The History of Sexuality*, Volume II', in P. Rabinow (ed.), *The Foucault Reader*. London

    (1986b) *The Use of Pleasure*. The History of Sexuality, Volume II, trans. R. Hurley. London

Freudenberg, K. (1990) 'Horace's satiric program and the language of contemporary theory in *Satires* 2.1', *AJPh* III. 187–203

Gamel, M. (1989) '*Non sine caede*: Abortion politics and poetics in Ovid's *Amores*', *Helios* 16. 183–206.

Gasché, R. (1987) 'Of aesthetic and historical determination', in Attridge, Bennington and Young (1987)

Goodyear, F.R.D. (1965) *Incerti auctoris Aetna*. Cambridge

Greene, G. and Kahn, C. (eds.) (1985) *Making a Difference: Feminist Literary Criticism*. London

Griffin, J. (1985) *Latin Poets and Roman Life*. London

Habermas, J. (1987) *The Philosophical Discourse of Modernity*. Cambridge

Hallett, J.P. (1973) 'The role of women in Roman elegy: counter-cultural feminism', *Arethusa* 6. 103–24

    (1977) '*Perusinae glandes* and the changing image of Augustus', *AJAH* 2. 151–71

    (1989) 'Female homoeroticism and the denial of reality in Latin literature', *Yale Journal of Criticism* 3. 209–27

Halperin, D.M. (1990) *One Hundred Years of Homosexuality and Other Essays on Greek Love*. London

Halperin, D.M., Winkler, J.J. and Zeitlin, F.I. (eds.) (1990) *Beyond Sexuality: The Construction of Erotic Experience in the Ancient Greek World*. Princeton

Heath, S. (1982) *The Sexual Fix*. London

Henderson, J.G.W. (1989) 'Satire writes "woman": *Gendersong*', *PCPhS* 35. 50–80

Hubbard, M. (1974) *Propertius*. London

Kennedy, D.F. (1992) '"Augustan" and "anti-Augustan": reflections on terms of reference', in A. Powell (ed.), *Roman Poetry and Propaganda in the Age of Augustus*. Bristol

Kermode, F. (1966) *The Sense of an Ending*. Oxford

Kundera, M. (1975) *Laughable Loves*, trans. S. Rappaport. London.

    (1984) *The Unbearable Lightness of Being*, trans. M.H. Heim. London

Lakoff, G. and Johnson, M. (1980) *Metaphors We Live By*. Chicago

Lee, G. (1974) '*Otium cum indignitate*: Tibullus 1.1', in A.J. Woodman and D.A. West (eds.), *Quality and Pleasure in Latin Poetry*. Cambridge

    (1990) *Tibullus: Elegies*. Leeds

Lentricchia, F. and McLaughlin, T. (eds.) (1990) *Critical Terms for Literary Study*. Chicago

Lyne, R.O.A.M. (1980) *The Latin Love Poets from Catullus to Horace*. Oxford

MacMullen, R. (1982) 'Roman attitudes to Greek love', *Historia* 31. 484–502

McKeown, J.C. (1979) 'Augustan elegy and mime', *PCPhS* 25. 71–84

    (1989) *Ovid: Amores. Text, Prolegomena and Commentary. Volume II: A Commentary on Book One*. Leeds

Moi, T. (1985) *Sexual/Textual Politics: Feminist Literary Theory*. London

Myerowitz, M. (1985) *Ovid's Games of Love*. Detroit

Pichon, R. (1902) *De sermone amatorio apud Latinos elegiarum scriptores*. Paris

Price, S.R.F. (1990) 'The future of dreams: from Freud to Artemidorus', in Halperin, Winkler and Zeitlin (1990)

Pucci, P. (1978) 'Lingering on the threshold', *Glyph* 3. 52–73

Randall, J.G. (1979) 'Mistresses' pseudonyms in Latin elegy', *LCM* 4. 27–35

Sayre, H. (1990) 'Performance', in Lentricchia and McLaughlin (1990)

Shepherd, W.G. (1985) *Propertius: The Poems*. Harmondsworth

Smith, K.F. (1913) *The Elegies of Albius Tibullus*. New York

Stahl, H.-P. (1985) *Propertius: 'Love' and 'War'. Individual and State under Augustus*. Berkeley

Sullivan, J.P. (1976) *Propertius: a Critical Introduction*. Cambridge

Veyne, P. (1976) *Le Pain et le cirque: sociologie historique d'un pluralisme politique*. Paris

    (1978) 'La famille et l'amour sous le Haut-Empire romain', *Annales (ESC)* 33. 35–63

    (1985) 'Homosexuality in ancient Rome', in P. Ariès and A. Béjin (eds.), *Western Sexuality*, trans. A. Forster. Oxford

    (1987) 'The Roman Empire', in P. Ariès and G. Duby (eds.), *A History of Private Life. I: From Pagan Rome to Byzantium*. London

    (1988) *Roman Erotic Elegy. Love, Poetry, and the West*, trans. D. Pellauer. Chicago

White, H. (1978) *Tropics of Discourse: Essays in Cultural Criticism*. Baltimore

Williams, G. (1968) *Tradition and Originality in Roman Poetry*. Oxford

Winkler, J.J. (1990) *The Constraints of Desire: The Anthropology of Sex and Gender in Ancient Greece*. London

Wyke, M. (1987a) 'Written women: Propertius' *scripta puella*', *JRS* 77. 47–61

    (1987b) 'The elegiac woman at Rome', *PCPhS* 33. 153–178

    (1989a) 'Mistress and metaphor in Augustan elegy', *Helios* 16. 25–47

    (1989b) 'Reading female flesh: *Amores* 3.1', in A. Cameron (ed.), *History as Text*. London

Zeitlin, F.I. (1990) 'The poetics of *erōs*: nature, art and imitation in Longus' *Daphnis and Chloe*', in Halperin, Winkler and Zeitlin (1990)

General index

Index of passages discussed

(Major discussions are indicated by **bold** type)